Earth Angels
& MAGIC MOMENTS
are Everywhere

by
Nicholas Boothman

Copyright © 2024 Nicholas Boothman
The scanning, uploading, and distribution of this book without
permission is a theft of the author's intellectual property. If you
would like permission to use material from the book (other than
for review purposes), please contact info@nicholasboothman.com
Thank you for your support of the author's rights.

ISBN: 978-0-9958581-1-4
Second printing January 2025

When one door closes, another door opens, but often we look so long and so regretfully at the door that closed that we don't see the one that opened.

Alexander Graham Bell
INVENTOR OF THE TELEPHONE

Boothman is Dale Carnegie for a rushed era.
The New York Times

Training the New York SuperCops includes daily discussions on the works of Aristotle, H. G. Wells, and Nicholas Boothman.

The New Yorker

Contents

CHAPTER 1: UNLUCKY OR WHAT? 11

CHAPTER 2: BUS STOP. BUS GO 17

CHAPTER 3: THE ILLUSIONS OF CHANCE 23

CHAPTER 4: THE EXPECTATION EFFECT 25

CHAPTER 5: THE STRANGER IN THE STORM 29

CHAPTER 6: IN PRAISE OF SPEAKING UP 33

CHAPTER 7: THE ANGEL ON MAIN STREET 47

CHAPTER 8: BUT, I DON'T TALK TO STRANGERS 49

CHAPTER 9: THE THREE SECOND RULE 61

CHAPTER 10: AN ANGEL ON SKID ROW 65

CHAPTER 11: THE STRANGER CHALLENGE 71

CHAPTER 12: A WORLD OF OPPORTUNITY 73

CHAPTER 13: WHO ARE THESE STRANGERS? 75

CHAPTER 14: AN ANGEL AT THE GAS STATION 81

CHAPTER 15: THE ART OF THE INTRODUCTION 91

CHAPTER 16: ASSUMING RAPPORT 95

CHAPTER 17: YOU CALL THE SHOTS 103

CHAPTER 18: THE HOPE RESTORERS 115

CHAPTER 19: MESSAGES IN THE MAKING	123
CHAPTER 20: EARTH ANGELS IN THE MAKING	131
CHAPTER 21: HELP ME FIND MY PURPOSE	137
CHAPTER 22: THE GREAT DEBATE	143
CHAPTER 23: AN UNEXPECTED DEPARTURE	161
CHAPTER 24: THE VERDICT	169
CHAPTER 25: A PURPOSE QUEST	173
CHAPTER 26: PURPOSE STATEMENTS	177
CHAPTER 27: A VERY MAGIC MOMENT	191
EPILOGUE	197
ACKNOWLEDGEMENTS	201
ABOUT THE AUTHOR	203

The stories in this book are inspired by real-life events.

It was a crisp March morning on March 8th, 2009, in New York City. I was on the last day of a twenty-city tour appearing on morning network TV shows to promote the release of my book, How to Make Someone Fall in Love with You in 90 Minutes or Less.

After returning to my hotel and changing, I decided to go for a walk. As I strolled down Fifth Avenue, I wondered how my book would be received and longed for a sign that the two years I spent researching and writing it was worthwhile.

The book opens with a quote by Luciano De Crescenzo, a famous Italian writer and director: "We are each of us angels with only one wing, and we can only fly by embracing one another." The word angel comes from the Greek word 'angelos', meaning messenger.

Feeling the need to sit quietly and reflect, I noticed Saint Patrick's Cathedral at Fifth and Fifty-First. Its Gothic spires and stunning stained-glass windows beckoned me to enter. However, as soon as I walked in, a voice in my head said, 'No, not here. This is not for you.' The words were clear and unmistakable, and I felt a familiar shiver run down my spine.

I turned around and left, wondering why I had been so abruptly dismissed. Was it the tourist crowds, the ornate decorations, or something more intangible that didn't resonate with me? I didn't know, but I trusted my instincts.

Three blocks further up Fifth Avenue, I spotted another church. Passing through the door of Saint Thomas Church, I immediately felt at peace.

"Where shall I sit?" I whispered to myself. 'I know. I'm sixty-two. I'll sit in pew sixty-two'. I walked down the center aisle and found it. The church was empty. I went about ten feet in and sat down.

After fifteen minutes of quiet contemplation, seeking inspiration for my next book, I randomly grabbed a prayer book from the rack in front of me and started flipping through the pages. I wasn't looking for anything in particular, just browsing. And then, something inside the back cover caught my eye. There, handwritten in Portuguese, my second language, was a quote that made my heart skip a beat: "We are each of us angels with only one wing, and we can only fly by embracing one another."

I couldn't believe it. It was like the universe was sending me a message. "No one's going to believe this," I thought to myself, so I pulled out my BlackBerry and took a picture of it. I wanted proof that this was real.

Why am I sharing this with you? Because things like this have been happening to me all my life. Over and over, people have said, "Nick, it's amazing; why don't you write it down?"

Well, I listened, and I have. I've written it all down. And here it is – a collection of stories, experiences, and insights that I hope will inspire, amaze, and maybe even change the way you think about the world.

EARTH ANGELS & MAGIC MOMENTS

Chapter 1:
Unlucky or What?

You've met them. We all have. Those people who always seem to be singing the same sad song: "I'm so unlucky." They'll regale you with tales of woe: the parking ticket, the missed flight, the job that slipped through their fingers. But is it really just bad luck? Or is there something else going on?

I've met plenty of people who say, "I'm unlucky." But if you look closely, you'll find luck has nothing to do with it; they're just really good at making really bad decisions and carrying them out really well. I know this from personal experience. Been there. Done that.

Or maybe they're not unlucky at all. Maybe they're just not paying attention to the opportunities that are right in front of them. Or maybe they're stuck in a pattern of negative thinking that's attracting more bad luck into their lives.

Of course, there are real tragedies and challenges in this world that are beyond our control—unexpected illnesses, natural disasters, and heartbreaking losses. That's not what we're talking about here. Instead, we're diving into the realm of serendipity, synchronicity, and epiphany—those magical moments when the universe opens new doors.

We've all experienced them: running into an old friend in a foreign country, stumbling upon a book that changes our perspective, or receiving an unexpected phone call that leads to a new career path. These "Earth Angels and Magic Moments" are more than just happy accidents. They're reminders that we're not alone, that there's a larger web of connection and meaning that weaves our lives together, nudging us toward our highest potential, and encouraging us to trust in the natural flow of life.

And the best part? They are available to everyone, regardless of their circumstances. They're not reserved for the lucky or the privileged. They're a universal language, spoken directly to our hearts, reminding us that we're part of a larger, more mysterious whole.

The term "angel" originates from the Greek word

"angelos," meaning messenger, and fittingly, earth angels aren't celestial beings with wings and halos. They're flesh-and-blood humans who show up at precisely the right time and present us with the next step forward (like bizarrely scribbling a message in a prayer book in Manhattan). The trouble is that most people either refuse to accept this, or don't know how to recognize them, or don't know how to connect the dots.

Earth Angels are the whispers of possibility, the nudges towards your best self. They're the reminders that you're not alone. That even when things look dark, there's a light, a guiding hand, a moment of pure magic waiting around the corner. They are proof that even in a world filled with chaos, there's a constant stream of hope, a steady flow of guidance. And all you have to do is open your heart and listen. Because these angels? They're here to help. They're here to guide. They're here to remind us that we're all in this together.

"Magic Moments" is just a lighthearted collective name for those spontaneous, serendipitous experiences that bring unexpected joy, insight, or opportunity into our lives. These moments can take many forms, from chance encounters and surprising coincidences to sudden epiphanies and inspired ideas. They often appear when we least expect them, yet somehow, they always seem to arrive exactly when we need them most. By embracing the presence of earth angels and the power of magic moments, we can tap into a deeper sense of connection, purpose, and wonder, and discover that the universe is always guiding us towards our highest good.

If you dismiss these moments as bunkum and demand proof they exist, you're going to find yourself out of luck—you can't cram miracles down people's throats. Accept them as a natural part of the universe's flow, and they'll soon feel as natural as gravity.

You can find plenty of attempts from different groups around the world to explain these phenomena. Hindus, quantum physicists, economists, skeptics, Carl Jung, and everyday spiritual folk all make their own cases for them—but in the absence of concrete proof, these are just opinions.

I'm not here to convince you. I'm not here to preach. I'm here to tell you the stories. The ones nobody can explain. The ones that defy logic.

Then, you be the judge. You decide. You decide if it's real. You decide if it's possible. You decide if you believe. Because in the end, that's all that matters. Your truth.

Chapter 2:
Bus Stop. Bus Go

Rush Mitchell, a thirty-four-year-old guy with a brain that worked like a super-fast calculator, always figuring things out, always wanting things to be neat and tidy, to go exactly as planned, suddenly found himself with a big fat zero in the job department, and a whole lot of nerves, because the rejections kept piling up, one after another, and he started to feel like maybe he was just plain unlucky, or maybe, even worse, like he was just… finished, like he didn't fit anymore.

His job, the one he thought he was good at, the one he thought was safe, was gone, snatched away by those AI robots, and it wasn't just his job, it was the whole industry, changing so fast he couldn't keep up, and he felt old, like a dinosaur in a world that didn't need dinosaurs anymore.

As he stood at the bus stop, shivering in the cold, he couldn't help but feel like the universe was conspiring against him. He had just missed the bus, and now he was stuck waiting for the next one.

But then, out of nowhere, he saw her.

A woman, with piercing green eyes and long, curly brown hair sitting on a bench, typing away on her laptop, fingers flying like she was in a race, and she looked busy, real busy, but also, she looked familiar, like he'd seen her somewhere before, and it was driving him crazy, because his brain, usually so good at remembering things, was drawing a blank.

He felt drawn to her, and as he sat down beside her on the bench, she looked up and smiled. He smiled back, and they struck up a conversation that flowed easily, like they had known each other for years. They talked about jobs, hiking, and life in general, but he couldn't shake the feeling that there was something more to this chance encounter.

As they chatted, he discovered that she was a career coach, specializing in helping people navigate the changing job market. It was a coincidence that seemed too good to be true, especially given his own recent struggles.

But as he looked into her eyes, he felt a sense of hope that he hadn't felt in weeks. It was as if fate had brought them together, and he felt a deep sense of gratitude for missing that bus. It had turned out to be a lucky break, one that might just change the course of his life.

As the bus rumbled to a stop, Rush stood up to leave, feeling lighter, freer. "Good luck with your job search," the woman said, "Remember, sometimes you need to take a leap of faith to find what you're looking for."

And with that, she vanished into the crowd, leaving Rush with a sense of wonder and a renewed sense of purpose. He never got her name, but her words seared themselves into his brain, refusing to let go.

Rush took a deep breath, feeling the spark of determination ignite within him. He was done playing it safe, done waiting for opportunity to come knocking. It was time to take control, to seize the day and make his own luck. The stranger's words echoed in his mind as he set out on a new path, one that would lead him down a road of twists and turns, triumphs and setbacks.

Rush expanded his job search. He networked with people in his industry, attended job fairs, and even considered freelance work.

One day, while volunteering at a local non-profit organization, Rush met representatives from a healthcare company. They were impressed by his skills and experience, and invited him for an interview.

He was hesitant at first, but something about the company's mission resonated with him. He nailed the interview and was offered a position as a program manager, overseeing community outreach initiatives.

It was a role he never could have planned or imagined, but it aligned perfectly with his passions and skills. Rush was thrilled to be working for a company that shared his values, and he was grateful for the stranger's advice that had set him on this path.

The job proved to be a game-changer for Rush, bringing a sense of purpose and fulfillment that had eluded him. It was a powerful reminder that life's biggest blessings often emerge from unexpected people in unexpected places, and that sometimes, all it takes is a few simple words.

EARTH ANGELS & MAGIC MOMENTS

Chapter 3:
The Illusions of Chance

Lucky breaks that seem to come out of nowhere are often the result of your own intentional choices.

First. The way you explain your experiences to yourself, your self-talk, has a profound impact on your decisions, your health, and your happiness. Telling yourself that you're always unlucky, that you're not worthy, or that things will never change can create a self-fulfilling prophecy. But there's a flip side: when you talk in the positive you become a magnet for opportunity, and those 'lucky breaks' start to show up with surprising regularity.

Second. your thoughts are a result of the company you keep. Spending time with people who radiate a positive outlook is the single most critical factor in your future fortune. Hang out with three confident people, and you'll probably be the fourth. Hang out with three complainers, and chances are you'll be the fourth. Hang out with three millionaires, and who knows? Hang out with three cheats, thugs, or conspiracy theorists, and guess what?

Third. Your willingness to take risks and step out of your comfort zone gives you access to all kinds of growth. To quote Eleanor Roosevelt, the former first lady of the United States, "Do one thing every day that scares you. On the other side of that fear, opportunity awaits."

To a cautious person like Rush, Eleanor Roosevelt's advice might seem a bit strange. After all, fear is a smart way to keep yourself safe from harm and risks. It's like a warning signal to be cautious. So, why would anyone want to do things that scare them on purpose? Our upbringing and education seem to contradict this notion. But, as Eleanor Roosevelt suggests, when we face our fears, we might find amazing opportunities waiting for us on the other side.

Chapter 4:
The Expectation Effect

Did you ever notice that everyone's a stranger until they're not? Each with their own struggles, and their own triumphs, and their own messages. And yet, it's often the people we least expect, the ones we pass on the street or sit next to us on a bench, who can have the most profound impact on our lives.

Life can be a messy, unpredictable, and downright scary place at times, but even in the midst of craziness, amazing things can happen. Strangers can become saviors, and chance encounters and lucky breaks can appear out of the blue.

The Expectation Effect, also known as the Pygmalion Effect, the Placebo Effect, or the Law of Attraction, is a powerful phenomenon where our thoughts and beliefs shape our reality. When we expect good things to happen, we're more likely to notice and seize them.

The Expectation Effect has been studied extensively in various fields, including psychology, neuroscience, education, and medicine. Numerous studies found that when we expect good things to happen, our bodies and minds respond in incredible ways.

Serendipity and expectation (2011): A study published in the Journal of Research in Personality found that people with a more open and curious mindset (i.e., those who expected to find interesting things) were more likely to experience serendipity.

Expectations and chance encounters (2018): A study published in the Journal of Social and Personal Relationships found that people who expected to have positive social interactions were more likely to experience chance encounters that led to new relationships. These studies suggest that having an open, curious, and growth-oriented mindset can increase the likelihood of experiencing serendipity.

When we expect positive outcomes, our brain's reward system is activated, releasing feel-good chemicals like dopamine that bring us joy and happiness. It's like our expectations can spontaneously rewire our brains for success!

Even if you're not open to magic moments, they can still surprise you. Your brain is always working behind the scenes, making connections and discovering new things, even when you're not thinking about it. And sometimes, things just happen by chance. You might get rescued, or influenced, or stumble upon a new career. These things can happen even if you're not attuned to them. It's just that they happen much more often when you are.

Chapter 5:
The Stranger in the Storm

The snowstorm of the century was bearing down on Jessie Stern as she white-knuckled the steering wheel, her car sputtering like a dying animal. The windshield wipers flailed wildly, but she managed to careen into a Taco Bell parking lot just as the employees were bailing out ahead of the storm.

"It was a Sunday evening, and no tow truck would come out until the storm passed," Jessie recalled, her voice still laced with the fear of that night. "I was alone, stranded, and desperate."

But then, like an angel in the darkness, Sofia appeared. A Taco Bell employee with a heart of gold, Sofia took one look at Jessie's stricken face and knew she had to act.

"Hey, are you okay?" Sofia asked, her voice a warm

hug on a cold night.

As Jessie poured out her story, Sofia listened with a compassion that went beyond mere kindness. She saw something in Jessie that no one else did—a deep-seated vulnerability, a cry for help.

And then, Sofia made a decision that would change Jessie's life.

"Why don't you come home with me?" she asked, her eyes sparkling with warmth. "My family will make you welcome."

As the storm raged on outside, Jessie found herself enveloped in a sense of belonging she hadn't felt in years. Sofia's family took her in, fed her, and sheltered her from the tempest. They even fixed her car, getting her back on the road in no time.

But more than that, Sofia gave Jessie a gift that would stay with her forever—the gift of kindness, of compassion, of connection. As Jessie prepared to leave, Sofia's parting words echoed in her mind: "Remember, kindness has the power to transform everything. Expect it in unexpected places, share it with others, and always remember – you are never alone."

Jessie's encounter with Sofia was a turning point, a wake-up call to the transformative power of human connection. It reminded her that even in the darkest moments, there is always hope, always kindness, always a stranger willing to lend a helping hand.

Chapter 6:
In Praise of Speaking Up

The rewards of speaking up far outweigh the risks.

You're basically invisible until you speak up. Nobody really notices you're there until you say something. And then, suddenly, you're visible. People acknowledge your presence and start paying attention to what you're saying.

It's kind of like being in a meeting. You can sit there silently, and nobody will really notice you. But the moment you contribute to the conversation, people start looking at you, listening to what you have to say, and responding to your comments.

You Are a Genius Until You Open Your Mouth

And then there's that other thing: the benefit of the doubt. People tend to think you're a genius until you open your mouth. They assume you're intelligent and capable until you start talking. And then, well, they might realize that you're not as smart as they thought. Or maybe you'll surprise them and say something really insightful. Either way, speaking up changes everything.

Professor Thomas Harrell at the Stanford Business School spent twenty years looking for "the success factor" and concluded the number one identifiable predictor of success, across all realms of life, is something he called 'social extroversion'—the ability to speak up.

When was the last time you spoke up to a stranger? When was the last time you tried?

Even if you have to step out of your comfort zone for a moment, the life you encounter when you step back in again will be different from the life you were living before you plucked up the courage to speak up.

That said, we all know that feeling when you're sitting next to a stranger on a bus or standing awkwardly in an elevator and someone insists on talking to you when you're not in the mood. Most unwanted conversations can be politely avoided with a brief answer and a curt smile. If they still insist on talking, a few stronger words may be necessary.

Your instincts are important, as are the non-verbal clues you pick up. Someone reading a book or tablet, listening to headphones, or crossing their arms and legs is not inviting a conversation. Be sensitive to the fact that some people may have a history of obnoxious intrusions, so if your attempts at conversation aren't reciprocated, back away gracefully.

Hunt for Common Ground

Once you make the move and speak up, try to find some common ground. Common ground is the holy grail of talking to strangers. The moment you find it, you have a bond. The pressure is off and you can share your stories and your ideas and your casual chit chat.

The quicker you find things in common, the faster the connection. To do this, get them talking. The easiest way to get someone talking is to ask them what they think about something. If you're at a convention, ask them what they think about the transportation, the hotel, the hours, their first impressions of the place. "Is this your first trip? What's your initial impression?" "What do you think of the view from the observation deck?"—anything to get them going. Another rapport-creating question is "How did you end up here?" This is a story that everybody has to tell, and it's almost guaranteed to get a conversation started.

As you converse and work on finding that common ground, make sure to keep your conversation light and stay away from anything political, religious, or sexual. Make sure the other person does at least half of the talking. Remember to shut up and listen. Listen with your eyes and your ears.

Simply pay attention to what's being said and when the opportunity arises jump in and say it—as long as it is the truth. For example, if someone says, "I love the Caribbean." You can simply say, "wow, what a coincidence," "no kidding, I totally agree," and "I love it there too." And of course, you can add to the conversation by asking follow-up questions like "What's your favorite island?" and "Do you snorkel?"

Once you find common ground, you find direction and momentum, the comfort level expands, and you can start to relax a little. However, skip the step of finding common ground and you're playing with fire.

Ask Talk Show Host Questions

Talk Show hosts, interviewers and journalists have a formula for getting people to open up, they start with a statement about the occasion or the location, and follow it with an open question. Those are the ones that begin with *who, where, why, when, what* and *how*. On the flight to Las Vegas, Kira, a Canadian, asked Carl, a Norwegian, "Tell me about Oslo. I hear it's a fantastic place (a statement). If I only had 4 hours *what* should I see? (an open question)"

Simple. Now she has him talking. Kira knows the best way to keep him talking is by giving feedback, both physical and spoken. She gives physical feedback by nodding and looking interested, and spoken feedback with words like, "oh," "aha," "wow." Kira knows the best open-ended question of all is "tell me about?" And it's not even a question.

Talk to Someone New

Speak up. It doesn't matter where you do it. Talk to the person next to you in line. Talk to the person sitting next to you on the plane/bus/train. Take your toddler to a playground and talk with the other parents.

It's perfectly natural to remark about the weather, how busy it is, how long you waited. If the person responds, listen to what they have to say. Give feedback. Nod, smile or grunt.

NEVER give out your personal details without a really good reason.

In everyday situations at work and online we meet strangers as new clients and coworkers. In the new Gig economy where organizations contract with independent workers on a temporary basis, the ability to make human connections with all sorts of strangers is a survival skill. Same goes for the Sharing economy where you share your car, your home and even your clothes with total strangers. The booming Zoom economy, where freelancers, entrepreneurs, and work-from-home employees come together online, are real hotspots for random creative collisions with strangers. Even in relaxed social settings, talking to strangers is a great way to meet Earth Angels and find Magic Moment.

Bridge builders are Earth Angels who facilitate connections, foster relationships, and create opportunities for others to come together. They play a vital role in making magic moments happen by building bridges between people, ideas, and communities, facilitating meaningful interactions and collaborations.

By connecting dots and introducing individuals with complementary skills, interests, or passions, bridge builders spark innovative partnerships and foster inclusive environments. They nurture relationships, provide support, and offer guidance, helping others navigate unfamiliar terrain.

Bridge builders identify common ground, find creative solutions, and resolve conflicts, ensuring harmonious collaborations. In doing so, they ignite serendipity, synchronicity, and epiphanies, creating opportunities for unexpected connections and insights.

These master weavers of connections have a profound impact on our lives. They help us find our tribe, our support system, and our sense of belonging. With each new connection, our lives become richer.

Bridge Builders come in many forms. They might be mentors guiding us towards our dreams, friends introducing us to new experiences, or strangers becoming lifelong companions. Their gift is the ability to bring people together.

Become a Temporary Extrovert

Is it any wonder so many people are afraid to step out of their comfort zone? Or that on a daily basis, millions miss out on opportunities to grow by unwittingly creating irrational phobic responses to new situations.

Be it fear of embarrassment, losing control, rejection, loss of income or upbringing, we miss out by making unconscious split-second limiting decisions.

It only takes a few small steps to overcome the everyday risks that cause paralysis right on the threshold of taking action.

Here are seven simple tips for becoming a temporary extrovert.

1. say hello to a stranger or two throughout your day
2. notice the color of their eyes

3. Respectfully synchronize your body language with others
4. become a temporary talk-show host and ask "talk-show host" questions (a statement followed by an open question). "I hear Seattle's a fantastic place. If I only had 3 hours what should I see?" Or become a temporary news reporter with endless curiosity
5. nod and grunt—give physical and spoken feedback
6. make it about them: not you, listen to their hopes and dreams
7. find common ground

Start small and safe and grow from there.

Compliment Strangers

Japanese scientists cracked the code. Brain scans don't lie. Turns out, a simple compliment lights up the *exact same* pleasure center as cold, hard cash. Professor Sadato, at the National Institute for Physiological Sciences at Okazaki, saw it himself: praise wasn't just fluff; it was a social reward with the same punch as money. And the kicker? People worked better, opened up more, all thanks to a few sincere words.

In Toronto, Peter needed a suit big time for his

internship at Davies & Stern. He'd never owned anything professional in his life. Jeans and tees were his comfort zone. Now? He felt like an imposter before he even started. The charcoal gray suit felt alien, stiff, hanging in his closet like a constant reminder of the new world he was about to enter. He just hoped he wouldn't look like a complete rookie.

Then Sarah saw him. Down the hall. Her eyes widened. "Peter! Wow," she said, the words hitting him like a jolt. "That suit looks *amazing* on you." Suddenly, the doubt vanished. He felt taller, more confident. "Really?" he asked, a grin spreading across his face. "Seriously," she replied, leaning against the doorframe. "You look… like a million bucks."

Million bucks. That's exactly how he felt. Ready for anything.

Most people feel good when they get a compliment. Learning how to make a stranger feel good when you compliment them is especially important if you are looking to open new doors and grow your network.

Look them in the eye for a second and mean it. Don't expect a compliment in return. This isn't tennis.

If you do get one back however, receive it gracefully.

A sincere compliment about a hairstyle, an accessory, clothes or eyes is ok for most people but complimenting someone's character or performance will leave a lasting impression.

"I was skiing at the ski hill I work at and I blew by an older lady," Loretta emailed, "at the bottom she came up to me and said 'You're such an amazing skier, you are an inspiration to watch."

"Thank you kind lady, you made my day."

"When a stranger found out I worked for Hospice," Vikki writes, "he said 'you're an angel.' It made me feel proud and humble in the same moment."

Sunil writes, "after a two hour conversation with a stranger on intuition, he told me that the convo we had was THE most engaging one in his life, which he never would have had with any of his family or best of friends."

Warren's greatest compliment came from a homeless woman who greeted him when he walked by. "Thanks for talking to me like I'm a human being," she said. "I've greeted everyone who walked by an you're the only person who did not completely ignore me."

Jeff's a fire-fighter. His best compliment came from a mother at an infant medical call, "I had no idea someone like you would be so good with babies."

The world can be a hard place. Sharp edges. Cold shoulders. Then, out of nowhere, it happens. A voice cuts through the noise. "Hey, kid, nice drawing." Or, "That presentation? Nailed it." Simple words. But they land like a shot of pure adrenaline. Suddenly, the doubt fades. The shoulders relax. You stand a little taller. Where do those words come from? Sometimes, it feels like they're not just kindness. It feels… different.

Think about the times it's happened to you. The random stranger who says your laugh is infectious. The colleague who genuinely praises your idea in a tough meeting. The way that one teacher *saw* something in you that no one else did. Those words? They stick. They build. They can change the whole trajectory of your day, maybe even your life. It's more than just politeness. It's like a little spark, igniting something inside. A Magic Moment?

Maybe those sparks are intentional. Maybe there

are people walking among us, tuned into the frequencies of insecurity and doubt. And maybe, just maybe, they're the ones dropping these perfectly timed compliments, these little bombs of encouragement. Earth angels? Could be. Whatever they are, they wield a quiet kind of power. The power to lift us, to inspire us, sometimes even to make us laugh when we thought we couldn't. And in a world that often feels dark, those little glimmers of light? They're everything.

Chapter 7:
The Angel on Main Street

Holly Castillo's eyes scanned the unfamiliar streets of Port Hope, her one-year-old daughter Prudence securely strapped into the jogging stroller. Two months ago, they'd made the move for her husband's teaching job, leaving behind the comfort and security of their old life. As a stay-at-home mom, Holly felt isolated, uncertain, and stuck in a rut.

That's when the accident struck. The stroller's tire blew out, sending Prudence into a fit of wails. Holly's face burned with embarrassment as she struggled to calm her daughter. The townspeople seemed to be staring, judging her. It was the final straw. Port Hope was not going to work out.

But then, a guardian angel appeared. A young girl, with a kind face and a bike, pulled up beside them.

"Need some help?" she asked, her eyes sparkling with warmth. In a flash, she'd patched the tire and inflated it. As she worked, she spoke words that would change Holly's life: "This town may not be perfect, but it's got heart."

Holly felt a weight lift off her shoulders. The girl's kindness and humility struck a chord. She realized that her cynicism was a habit she'd developed over time, a shield to protect herself from disappointment. But in that moment, she saw the world with fresh eyes.

As they continued their jog, Prudence's giggles filled the air. Holly felt a sense of belonging she hadn't expected. "I definitely like Port Hope," she said, her feet clicking confidently on the sidewalk.

It was a small moment, but one that changed Holly's mind. Sometimes, it's the little things that can shift our perspective. A kind stranger, a helping hand, and suddenly, the world looks different.

But what about when the stakes are higher? When lives are at a crossroads, and the darkness seems overwhelming? That's when the angels appear, disguised as strangers, offering a lifeline.

Chapter 8:
But, I Don't Talk to Strangers

Late one snowy January afternoon in 2019, Eric Hogan looked up from the hunk of Krispy Kreme doughnut he was about to dunk into his coffee. That's when the chaos erupted.

Four noisy teenagers tumbled into the booth directly in front of him. Doughnuts in one hand, drinks and phones the other, knapsacks dangling from shoulders and elbows, they nudged and scrunched themselves in to the booth. Energetic. Absorbed. Radiant. Winter jackets off. Eric's eyes rolled heavenward. 'Just what I need.'

But as he watched the teens settle in, something shifted inside him. Curiosity got the better of him, and he stood up, counting to three in his head. It was a moment of reckoning, a choice between annoyance and engagement. Eric's eyes locked onto the teens, and he smiled to himself. 'This is about to get interesting.'

"Hi," he said quietly, standing a few feet away, not wanting to intrude. "I was just noticing you guys talking. You seem to be having a nice time, and I was wondering if I could ask you something?" They looked up, a little surprised, but not unfriendly. "I write a blog for the Newcastle Times, just little stories, and I was curious about something," he explained gently. "If that's okay?"

Fortunately, at that very moment the waitress squeezed by and said, "Need a top-up, Eric?"

"No, thank you, Sally, I'm all set." A small, familiar connection established. The boy, Ben, gave a little nod. "What's the story about?"

"Just about talking to people you don't know," Eric said softly. "How you feel about it."

A few quiet giggles. Some shrugs. Ben made room on the bench. "Want to sit?"

Eric asked their names, his voice calm. Selina and Anna, side-by-side. Ben and Lilly across from each other. They agreed he could record their conversation. A quiet click. Eric leaned in, a gentle interest in his eyes. He had a feeling there was a small, interesting story here, waiting to be heard.

"When was the last time you talked to a stranger?"

"Well right now I guess," Lilly said. Big laugh. "Ok. Yesterday at McDonalds."

Anna thought for a while then said. "I don't really know."

The other two said nothing.

"How do you feel about talking to strangers?" Eric asked.

Lilly replied again. "Sometimes it's weird because you don't really know who they are."

Anna said, "I know. Me and my mom were looking at stuff in a store and someone said 'I've tried that one before.' But she spoke to us first. But then it turned into a convo."

"So," Eric directed the question to Anna, "how do you feel about talking to strangers?"

"It's kind of like… I don't know."

Selina was staring at Anna. She glanced at Eric then

looked away. "I don't talk to strangers."

"Oh yes," Eric asked, "how come?"

Selina kept her eyes on Anna. "Because some of them are weird." Her voice went up at the end as if she was asking a question.

"How do you mean?" Anna asked.

"Because the last time a stranger came up to me, they tried to kidnap me." Anna bobbed her head a little and looked at the others. "For real." Selina insisted glaring at Anna. "At the mall. Some weirdo offered to buy me a doughnut. So, I don't talk to strangers now."

Ben lifted the mood. "Last time I talked to a stranger I was walking home and there was this old woman shoveling the snow at the end of her driveway so I helped her and we got talking."

Anna and Lilly laughed and called him a hero. They were warming up.

Selina turned slightly in Eric's direction but made no eye contact.

"It's not fair. It's all these rules about 'don't do drugs' and 'don't do alcohol' and 'don't do bullying' and 'don't talk to strangers' but there's nothing about treating people with respect." Selina sighed and rested both elbows on the table, palms and fingers splayed outwards. Then almost whispering, "why can't we accept somebody for who they are, even when they're different from us and we don't agree with them? Why can't we just treat people with respect? Why?"

"Hey," Eric said, "I'm sorry if I've upset you. I guess I'm doing exactly what you're talking about but it's not my intention to scare you. This isn't about you, or me. It's about 500 words to help people connect and make their lives easier, friendlier, safer. And even make a few magic moments."

Selina made eye contact with Eric for the first time. "Magic?"

"Magic moments. Sure." Eric said. "That's what can happen. Not the rabbit-out-of-a-hat kind. The real kind. The kind that leaves you feeling a little less alone in the world. The kind that reminds you that everyone has a story, a struggle, a moment of joy. Talking to strangers isn't some grand gesture. It's a small act of courage, a tiny leap of faith. But the rewards? They can be huge. A new friend. A vital piece of information. A moment of unexpected kindness that restores your faith in humanity. And sometimes, just sometimes, a connection so profound it feels like... well, like a little bit of magic walked into your ordinary day."

Anna and Ben nodded and smiled and Ben said, "Cool."

"Have you ever met a stranger and had something magic come from it?" Eric asked.

Lilly answered. "New friends."

Anna agreed. "Yeah. New friends."

"I didn't know any of these guys until we met," Selina said slurping-up the last of her shake.

Eric laughed out loud. "How did you start talking to each other?"

They were talking over each other now.

"Don't know," Lilly said.

Anna agreed. "We just started hanging out together and we sat with each other."

They gossiped about who introduced who and where and when.

"Could you stand in a line up and talk to a stranger?" Eric asked after a few moments.

"No. Could you?" Selina fired back.

"Yes and no," Eric said. "When I was growing up, I'd talk to pretty much anyone – within reason. But actually, I never really knew what to say." No-one spoke so Eric carried on. "I had this friend Bill. We were both about twelve and he could talk and talk to anyone anywhere. I used to think if I could just catch some of the stuff that comes out of his mouth and use it myself it would be great. But hey, it doesn't work that way."

Ben broke the silence. "I guess back then it was probably a lot safer because now it's dangerous." He looked around. "Sort of."

"I feel like because of the internet, I don't know," Lilly said. "I feel like back then people were nicer."

"More friendly." Ben nodded to the girls.

"Because they didn't have all the technology," Anna said

"And more respectful to people," said Lilly.

"More outgoing," added Anna

"For me, having a sister and being like me I find it easier to talk to someone because I don't care," Ben said. "For girls it's a little harder to talk to strangers because they're living in that fear of 'what if I get taken'."

"Do you think it should be a fear?" Eric asked the table.

"I feel like people shouldn't be as scared as we are," Anna said. "But I feel that people should be a little scared."

"Aware," Said Ben.

"Yes, aware of the things that could happen," Anna added.

"Do you wish you could talk to strangers?" Eric asked.

A resounding "Yes" from three of them.

"So, what's stopping you?" Eric said to Anna.

"I wish I could feel less scared; less awkward about it," Anna replied.

"Why bother," Selina snapped.

Eric stood up. "Thanks. Just one more thing. In my blog I'm asking readers to say something to a stranger at least once a day for a week and let me know how it goes. What do you think? Would any of you do that and text me how it went?"

Yes," Ben shrugged. "I will."

"Sure. I feel like when I'm walking down the street, I smile at people anyway," Lilly said. "I kind of 'mouth-hi' them. I don't really say it."

"Sure," Said Anna.

"Sorry," Selina said.

"Hey that's cool," Anna told her.

Eric asked their ages. Two of them were fourteen and two just turned fifteen. He asked which generation they thought they belonged to. Ben quickly replied, "Gen Z". For a moment they were thinking then Selina said. "We're teenagers."

All four of them took the challenge and texted their feedback.

Anna wrote: "Hangin' with my bestie & seein' her vibe with strangers made me realize talkin' to ppl ain't nothin'! But lol she can chat for hours & I'm over here like "wrap it up". Anyway, I had to take a leap & JUST DO IT. Opened up, let go my fears & didn't care what others thought. And honestly, I got some sick new info out of it"

Lilly wrote: "I went to Winners after school and two times I ask just customers about wearing wool. What was weird is that really I'm shy but I came out of myself more with strangers than with people I know."

Ben wrote: "Mr. Dodd, my gym teacher hates me and I really don't think I deserve this. When other kids compliment him, he smiles. I have decided to give him one complement a day so that I can get over my fear."

Selina wrote: "Omg I was at the supermarket and I said hi to this old dude collectin donations for Salvation Army and I threw in a buck and he starts chattin me up and I'm dyin but he's actually really cool and now I'm in a good mood lol."

Eric's blog sparked a heated debate, with some hailing his approach as a refreshing way to build confidence and social skills in teens, while others condemned it as reckless and potentially harmful. As for the teens who took Eric's challenge and started talking to strangers, the results were mixed. Some reported feeling empowered and making unexpected connections, while others felt uncomfortable or even scared. It became clear that there's no one-size-fits-all answer to this complex issue, and that the key to navigating stranger interactions lies in finding a balance between caution and openness.

And, what if the real danger isn't talking to strangers, but rather the fear and mistrust we instill in our kids? What if by shielding them from the unknown, we're also shielding them from potential connections and magic moments. Perhaps it's time to rethink the 'stranger danger' narrative and instead teach our kids to navigate the world with confidence, common sense, and curiosity?

Chapter 9:
The Three Second Rule

The longer you put something off, the harder it gets. But what if you could break the cycle of procrastination and seize the moment? Eric did just that at the donut store, using the three-second rule to spark a connection with the students. And it's exactly this kind of boldness that can help you tap into the power of earth angels and magic moments because:

- Earth angels often appear unexpectedly, and their presence can be fleeting.
- Magic moments are often brief and fragile.
- The three-second rule allows us to bypass our rational, cautious mind and tap into our intuitive, spontaneous nature.

Did you ever miss out on an opportunity because you were too slow off the mark? Or talk yourself out of doing something and then regret it later? If you just hang around wishing, waiting and hoping for something to happen, nothing ever will. You end up feeling bad because you talked yourself out of something or just plain chickened out. The more you hesitate, the more reason you have to beat yourself up for procrastinating. Sometimes you just have to go for it. The more you practice the easier it gets. For example:

Read the following three scenarios. Using the details of the situation along with your imagination decide what you would say. Come up with a conversational statement or two for each, and then follow it with an open question. One that begins with "Who," "What," "Why," "Where,"

"When," or "How." There are no right or wrong answers.

1. It's raining and as you leave the store several people are waiting under the awning for the rain to let up, because, like you, they have no umbrella. You are standing near someone and you say….

2. You're at work or at school and you walk outside for a break because it's a beautiful afternoon. You notice someone you don't know. You say….

3. You stop at a convenience store for a cup of coffee and notice someone you've seen around the campus getting ready to pour a cup too. You say….

Chapter 10:
An Angel on Skid Row

For Roger Martin, struggling with addiction and abandonment, his earth angel was Liam, a paramedic with a heart of gold. Liam saw beyond the surface, offering a helping hand, a listening ear, and a chance for Roger to reclaim his life.

In these moments, the power of human connection shines bright, illuminating a path forward. It reminds us that sometimes, all it takes is one person to believe in us, to make a difference, and to change the course of our lives forever.

An Angel on Skid Row

Roger Martin was addicted, abandoned, and wandering Manchester's downtown in the dark when a stranger pulled up beside him. He mistook the uniform for a police officer. What happened next changed Roger's life.

"I don't think you belong here," the man said.

Those words cracked Roger open like an egg. He'd said it to himself a hundred times. His hard shell was broken and his gentle heart was revealed.

Liam was a paramedic. "I don't know why I spoke to him. I'd seen him a few times and he just didn't fit in; I just knew he needed help."

They talked over coffee, and Liam learned that Roger had a son in Preston, less than 30 miles away. They hadn't spoken in 4 years: Roger was too ashamed. Liam got Roger a room for the night in a shelter and offered to meet him at the bus station and buy him a ticket to Preston the next day.

After some persuading, Roger gave Liam permission to call his son Andy. Liam contacted Andy and told him the plan.

"Life was never easy with dad." Andy told Liam. "He was a respected physics professor at Lancashire U. I used to idolize him but his obsession with work got him addicted to prescription pills and eventually I felt ashamed and angry. Mum left; I left, and he lost the house."

Liam's voice cracked as he spoke. "You have no idea what being abandoned really does to a human," he told Andy. "It's the constant questioning of your worth." It's the erosion of trust, the crumbling of faith in others and yourself. The nagging fear that you'll never be enough, that you'll always be left behind."

"But how could someone so brilliant fall so far?" Andy asked.

Liam's expression turned inward, his eyes clouding over. "Brilliance is a fragile thing, Andy," he said, his voice barely above a whisper. "It's a flame that burns brightly but can be blown out by the slightest breeze. Genius often comes with demons, Andy. The same minds that create and innovate are also prone to self-destruction. The pressure to constantly perform, the weight of expectation, the fear of failure... it can be crushing."

Liam's gaze drifted away, lost in a haze of memories. "Then there's the darkness lurking inside you. Shadows that haunt you and cling to you like shrouds. Mental illness, addiction, obsession... the list goes on."

His voice cracked, like a fault line splitting open. "I've seen it happen, Andy. The brightest stars burning out in a blaze of glory, leaving behind only ashes and what-ifs." Liam's eyes refocused; his gaze was piercing. "Brilliance is a double-edged sword. It can take you to dizzy heights, but it can also plunge you into unimaginable depths. And sometimes, no matter how hard you try, you can't escape the fall."

Liam got to the bus station ten minutes early unsure if Roger would actually show up but he was already there.

"Andy will meet you." Liam told him.

Roger's eyes shone with gratitude as he grasped the ticket. "You believe in me. That's life-changing," he said, savoring the weight of Liam's trust. "It makes me feel seen, heard, and valued. No one's believed in me for a long time. Not since...well, not since I stopped believing in myself."

Liam's gaze held Roger's, his words piercing deep. "Beliefs are just opinions, Roger. They are fragile and fickle. Faith is deeper than that, faith is trust and confidence. Faith in yourself is the spark that ignites the fire within you," Liam said. "It's a flame that no one can dim—except you."

Roger felt a glimmer of hope for the first time in years.

Chapter 11:
The Stranger Challenge

The results had been nothing short of astonishing. Anna, the introverted bookworm, found herself opening up to strangers in ways she never thought possible. Lilly, the shy and reserved one, discovered that talking to strangers was easier than she thought. Ben, the determined athlete, decided to take on his nemesis, Mr. Dodd, the gym teacher who seemed to hate him. And Selina, the free-spirited artist, struck up a conversation with an old dude collecting donations for the Salvation Army.

As they shared their experiences, the debate began. Some hailed Eric's challenge as a breakthrough, a way to build confidence and social skills in teens. Others condemned it as reckless, potentially putting vulnerable teens in harm's way.

But as the debate raged on, one thing became clear: there's no one-size-fits-all answer to this complex issue. The key to navigating stranger interactions lies in finding a balance between caution and openness. It's a delicate dance, one that requires empathy, self-awareness, and a willingness to take risks.

Eric's challenge had ignited a firestorm, but it had also sparked something more profound: a conversation about the power of human connection in a world where strangers are often seen as threats rather than opportunities.

As the teens reflected on their experiences, they realized that talking to strangers wasn't just about building confidence or social skills – it was about connection, empathy, and understanding. It was about recognizing that every stranger has a story, a perspective, and a humanity that's worth exploring.

And so, the challenge continued. The teens vowed to keep pushing past their fears, to keep seeking out new connections and experiences. They knew that the world was full of strangers, but they also knew that every stranger has the potential to become a friend, a mentor, or a kindred spirit.

Chapter 12:
A World of Opportunity

Life Doesn't Happen Without Talking to Strangers

Talking to strangers isn't just the right thing to do it's a matter of survival and a force of nature as old as humanity itself. Whatever it is you want in this life: a dream job, a great education or a crazy idea or a ticket to the World Cup—chances are you'll need a strangers help to get it. To understand this is to recognize one of life's simple truths: life doesn't happen without talking to strangers.

If you've ever been on the subway or in an elevator, you know the rules. Don't make eye contact, stay as far away from other people as you can, and whatever you do, don't talk to strangers.

But what if the rules are wrong?

The benefits of talking to strangers not only make

life more enjoyable and full of unforeseen opportunities but it also helps develop confidence and high self-esteem and puts an end to loneliness and isolation.

Surely, it's better to convince everyone that talking to the right strangers can not only make their lives safer, healthier, and more fun, it's pretty much the only guaranteed way to meet new people.

It is human nature that people like people like themselves: that birds of a feather flock together. We enjoy the company of people who share a common world-view, look the same, enjoy the same activities, and speak the same language as ourselves. We join clubs to be with others like us and we enjoy working with them when we play by their rules.

Chapter 13:
Who Are These Strangers?

Some cultures have no word for strangers because the people they haven't yet met are assumed to be friends. In our culture, though, the people we haven't yet met are assumed to be strange.

Then, there are the countries where it is taboo to talk to strangers. In the West, it's very common to say "Hi" to strangers as you walk in the park or wait at a station, but try that in Asian cultures, and you'll be greeted with raised eyebrows unless you know the person.

In the US, yes, we actually talk to strangers, but we just throw out the easy "Hi" and "How are you" with no real meaning. People don't really care how you are. It's just a gesture, a social thing.

If you walk around in Scandinavian countries

saying "Hi" to strangers on the street or in the park, they might regard you suspiciously or think there might be something wrong with you mentally.

Yet, the pandemic of 2020 made us realize just how much we crave the company of strangers. But just who are these strangers?

Familiar Strangers

Close your eyes and picture some of the strangers you see frequently but never speak to. The ones you sit or stand next to on the bus or train every day or pass by at the office or school. You see them regularly and they see you too. You recognize them; you might even nod or smile or "mouth-Hi" them, but you never actually speak to them. You might walk past a shop every day on the way to work, a shop that you've never been into but you see the shopkeeper every morning, so you smile and nod at each other. We call these people Familiar Strangers.

Consequential Strangers

Now think about some of the strangers you have interactions with as you go about your life who aren't family or close friends. We call them Consequential Strangers. It's a term coined by Professor Karen Fingerman in her book Consequential Strangers. These are your neighbors, coworkers, store clerks, local police officers, or members of a religious or community group. They're tradespeople like the butcher, the baker, your mechanic, the fresh-fruit lady at the market. While we take them for granted, they can enrich our lives in ways we never imagined. For one, job opportunities and lucky breaks most likely come from Consequential Strangers.

When Alfred Hamilton lost his job as vice president of a savings and loan company he didn't lose his talent for making connections. Within three weeks he had gathered the names of 134 people who might be able to help him in his job search; he had met with thirty-seven of them and received three job offers.

Alfred's plan had two steps. First, he tried to have a face-to-face meeting with whomever he could; second, he got two referrals from everyone he met with. Starting with his consequential contacts, he phoned and said, "I want to talk to you about something. I am looking for a job. I'm not calling to ask you for a job, but rather two names of people I can contact. As you know, I have . . . [here he lets slip his ten-second commercial, plus his credentials]. I'd like to be able to use your name as an introduction, not a reference. That's all I want."

Total Strangers

Then there are Total Strangers: people you've never even seen or bumped into yet.

Perfect Strangers

And Perfect Strangers, people who you've maybe heard of or read about who you know can help you "perfect" your goals and dreams. When Elon Musk was in his early twenties, he'd phone the Perfect Strangers he'd read about in magazines or seen on TV and ask them out to lunch.

Danger Strangers

And then there are the Danger Strangers, people who, right or wrong, set off your fight or flight response the moment you see them. If you've watched enough episodes of Law and Order, seen enough gangster movies or cheap reality TV, or played enough games of Grand Theft Auto you probably have a bit of a distorted idea of who you can trust at first sight and who you can't.

The world isn't a TV show or a video game; it's a reality. Most parts of all towns and cities are safe, but your street smarts and common sense should tell you don't walk alone down dark alleys at night, don't flash wads of cash in public, and don't get drunk in places you don't know. Do make an effort to blend in to your surroundings as much as possible, do draw in the support of total strangers—people of your choice—if you feel unsafe, do use your common sense, and above all, do trust your gut: listen to it, and if something doesn't feel right, get out of there.

The Biggest Miracle of All

We need the emotional input of other humans as much as we do the air we breathe and the food we eat. Deprive us of it, and we will wither and die, just as surely as if we were deprived of food and fresh air.

But, when people come together, joy and knowledge can be shared, love and hope can be found, food can be grown, diseases can be cured, the environment can be saved and miracles can happen every day, every hour, every minute—because the biggest miracle of all is you.

So what's holding you back?

Chapter 14:
An Angel at the Gas Station

The sun was setting over the Western Cape, casting a golden glow over the desolate landscape. But for Miriam and Mark, the beauty of the Garden Route was lost in a sea of anxiety. The empty gas tank light had been taunting them for miles, its ominous glow a constant reminder of their vulnerability.

They'd been warned about the dangers of driving in South Africa—the carjackings, the stabbings, the poverty-stricken desperation that lurked around every corner, especially in the open countryside. But Mark had been confident, convinced that they could make it to the next town before running out of fuel.

Miriam's intuition had screamed at her to listen, to turn back while they still could. But she'd silenced that voice, trusting Mark's judgment instead. Now, as the darkness deepened and the silence between them grew thicker, she couldn't shake the feeling that they'd made a terrible mistake.

The last town was 30 miles behind them, a distant memory in the rearview mirror. The next one lay 15 miles ahead, a promise of safety and salvation. But as they rounded a bend, the engine sputtering on fumes, Miriam's heart sank. They were running on empty, literally and figuratively.

And then, like a beacon in the darkness, they saw it —a sign that read "Fuel and Oil: 5 miles." Mark exhaled a sigh of relief, but Miriam's fear didn't dissipate. They were still miles from safety, still vulnerable to the dangers that lurked in the shadows.

As they coasted towards the gas station, their hearts pounding in unison, Miriam couldn't help but wonder – would they make it in time? Or would the darkness consume them, leaving them stranded and helpless in the vast expanse of the African night?

The place had seen better days. Lights were out on the pumps and the sign sprayed on the repair bay door said "closed." But lights were on around the side, near the back.

Miriam pulled onto the forecourt and up to a rusty, broken gas pump. They both got out. "This doesn't look good." Mark said.

"No, it doesn't. This is serious," Miriam said. "This place is filthy and disgusting and dangerous." Her eyes darted toward a creaking sound from the side of the building.

An old African man in greasy overalls shuffled out from a side door. A tall young woman in a red, black, and white African dress carrying a baby followed him out and stood under the light.

The old man came up to the car.

"Sorry lady. No petrol."

Miriam slumped against the Golf. "Jesus. Now what?"

"Ya madam," The old man tutted. "Jesus indeed. If you want petrol you need a miracle. There's been no petrol here for two years now."

"Grandpa."

"It's alright Tilly."

"No, Grandpa, look." The girl holding the baby

pointed to the road.

In the twilight, an old green farm truck with half a dozen men in the back rolled on to the forecourt.

"Go inside Tilly. You know what to do. Go now."

The truck revved up, scrunched into gear, and stopped by the repair bay door. The driver got out. He was short and fit, with brown skin, brown hair, and brown eyes. He sidled over to Miriam, glaring at her. The old man stood back. The rest of the men hopped down from the back of the truck and surrounded them.

"Well, what have we here today?" The driver spoke very slowly. "Tourists. Oh, dear me. Bad news, indeed. For you." He stepped inside Miriam's personal space. She tried to back up but was jammed against the car. "What are you doing out here lady? At night? In the dark?" Miriam was terrified. The man backed off, walked around the Golf and met Mark face-to-face. "Fuel mismanagement, eh?"

Mark nodded.

"Is that it?" The driver pushed into him. "Assuming the engine has enough fuel to continue running," the man snorted. "Shame on you. Bad management?"

"Yes." Mark stuttered.

The other men started laughing.

The driver turned to face his men. "Right. Grab them. Put them in the truck."

Mark was ready to go down fighting. Miriam's legs were shaking so badly that she thought she might pass out.

"Tilly," the old man yelled. "Now."

A light came on over the service bay door. The door thumped into life and started to open upwards, revealing three large drums with AVGAS stenciled on the side.

The old man slapped the driver on the back and they burst out laughing.

"Right then," said the driver, smiling. "Load them up, guys."

The men disappeared behind the truck and began rolling the heavy drums of aviation fuel onto the liftgate.

The driver turned to Miriam, then Mark. "I'm Cheech; this is my dad." These are my guys. I'm a crop sprayer. That's my fuel." He flashed a huge, toothy grin at Mark. "Fuel. You know what that is, eh?"

"You are terrible man," the old man said, hiding his laugh with his palm. "Scaring them to death."

"They need scaring to death."

"Norman," Cheech called out to a beefy teenager in a red shirt. "Put some truck petrol into this thing here."

Tilly came over, and Cheech wrapped his arm around her waist.

"Tilly-girl, you should have seen their faces."

Miriam and Mark were hanging on to each other, confused and still in shock. Then Miriam pushed Mark away.

"You're a fool," she said, "and so am I for listening to you. I should have listened to myself."

"We're okay aren't we," Mark replied.

"All I know is it's dark and it's dangerous and I'm scared out of my mind."

"I ran out of gas once in my aircraft." Cheech said. "I managed to land and I blamed my guys for overloading her. But it wasn't their fault it was mine. I got such a shock I promised it would never happen again. Ever. I wanted you to have a shock too."

Miriam looked at him. This crazy little man with his over-generous lips and big-hearted eyes. She didn't know whether to hate him or love him for what he just said.

"When I stopped blaming other people, I began to take responsibility for my actions and my choices. And you know what? Good things started to happen. I felt more confident, and more at peace. I think it's because when we stop blaming others, we start to focus on what we can control."

Norman emptied the five-gallon container of petrol into the Golf, and Cheech went off to supervise his men. He stopped abruptly and came back. He offered his hand to Miriam. She did nothing. Cheech waited. Miriam put out her hand; she thought he was going to shake it but he just held it lightly.

"Lady, life is too valuable to waste and too priceless to replace. You are responsible for your own life. Not him. Not nobody else. You blame him; you learn nothing."

Cheech smiled and released her hand. He set off back to check on the loading.

"See over there," the old man said to Mark. He pointed to the glowing dome of light on the horizon. "Those lights? That's the city—just ten more miles. See that smoke just there? Two miles."

"That's Skolly Boys," Tilly said, hoisting her child from one hip to the other. "Hoodlums and hijackers."

"Look out for bricks on the road," the old man said. "Go around them and don't stop for any reason."

Tilly picked up on the fear in Miriam's eyes and winked at her. Miriam caught it and sucked in her breath.

"Cheechy." Tilly called over to the truck. "Come here now, my big boy." Cheech waited as the last barrel was secured on the truck, then went over to her.

Tilly wrapped her arm around his waist. "You take them past those Skolly Boys; do you hear me?"

"Ya boss," he said saluting her with his free hand.

"Make sure they're safe." Tilly slapped his backside.

As she watched them, something enormously spiritual broke inside Miriam: a sudden moment of revelation, like they were all actors in a play. Like it was all planned. Like they were never in danger. She slumped down sideways onto the driver's seat, feet on the forecourt and felt a peace that seemed too good to be true. And she wept tears of pure love.

The men were all back in the truck and the Avgas was safely secured. Tilly came over and stood in front of Miriam. When Miriam looked up, Tilly offered her her hands. They were graceful, patient hands—not at all what Miriam expected. She took them and stood up.

Their eyes locked. Strangers in the night.

"Thank you," said Miriam.

"How much do I owe you?" Mark asked Cheech.

"It's on the house, eh, Dad?"

"This miracle's on Jesus," the old man replied. "I think."

Chapter 15:
The Art of the Introduction

The scene was set—a crowded convention center, the hum of conversation, and the faint scent of freshly brewed coffee. It was the perfect storm for networking, but for those who shied away from strangers, it could be a daunting task.

That's where the power of introduction came in. Researchers called it a "closed field setting," where the expectation was clear – you were there to meet people. And with a third-party introduction, the ice was broken, and the conversation flowed effortlessly.

But it wasn't just about being introduced; it was about how you were introduced. A well-crafted introduction can make all the difference. It was like a personal recommendation, a seal of approval that said, "This person is worth talking to."

So, how do you make a memorable introduction? Ask your host or mutual friend to do the honors, but don't leave it to chance. Give them a script, a brief rundown of who you are and what you do. Make it interesting, make it memorable.

"Ainslie, this is Adrian. He's one of Cape Town's leading church designers" was a far cry from "Ainslie, this is Adrian. He got soaked coming here, didn't you, Adrian?" The difference was stark – one introduction sparked curiosity, the other inspired awkward laughter.

In the world of strangers, an introduction was more than just a courtesy; it was a lifeline, a bridge that connected two worlds. And with the right introduction, the possibilities were endless.

Open and Closed Fields

It doesn't always work like that, though. At times you will see someone you'd like to meet in a public "open field setting," like an airport, shopping mall, supermarket, or a Krispy Kreme doughnut shop. For most of us, this can be daunting.

No matter what the situation, you can approach

strangers you're attracted to in two ways: the direct approach and the indirect approach.

The Direct Approach

For most of us, this is scary. Unless you're a movie star, on the Blue Jays baseball team, or a notoriously wealthy bachelor, it takes a lot of guts to approach a stranger and start talking. But sometimes it's act now or never see the person again and the strength of your feelings overwhelms you and compels you to act.

When you are unsure, use the three-second rule to overcome hesitation. One, two, three; here we go.

The goal is to simply greet, nod, or acknowledge a few strangers while you're out and about.

Try it for yourself. Start small, choose strangers who aren't intimidating in any way: a barista, a sales assistant, or a friendly looking old person. You're not going to start a conversation unless the opportunity comes up—if you do, that's a bonus.

You are creating a new habit, with "one, two, three" as your trigger. Practice, practice, practice—just do it. The key point is that you'll get comfortable breaking the ice and taking action. Give it a shot.

Chapter 16: Assuming Rapport

Imagine walking into a crowded room, scanning the sea of faces, and locking eyes with someone who sparks your interest. You take a deep breath, stride confidently towards them, and without so much as a hello, launch into a conversation as if you've known them all your life.

This indirect approach is how socially gifted people make most of their initial connections. They simply turn up next to or in front of the person they want to connect with, synchronize with them, and carry on as if they've known them for years.

Think of your local priest, rabbi, mullah, or some other religious leader; 99 percent of the time they just assume they know you and get on with the business at hand. It's one of the skills you learn as you get older and more seasoned at connecting with other people—but there's no reason you can't assume rapport at any age.

As infants we are great at assuming rapport. But then, somewhere between toddlerhood and childhood, we somehow manage to become intimidated by others for a few decades. Then thirty or forty years later, the lucky ones revert back to the open, friendly innocence of childhood.

Assuming rapport is a subtle, less-intrusive way to connect with a person you're interested in. It's less emotionally risky than the direct approach because it doesn't require any kind of introduction and outright request. You simply turn up, note something interesting that's going on at that moment, and begin your conversation in the middle.

How to Assume Rapport

Any of the following types of statements, questions, or compliments will do to get you started:

- An open question (i.e. one that can't be answered by a simple yes or no), such as "So, what have you heard about this movie?"

- An occasion/location statement, which refers to what's going on around you as well as to where you happen to be (e.g. the market). For example, "At last, fresh peaches."
- An occasion/location statement, followed by an open question: "At last, fresh peaches. How can I tell if it's ready to eat?"
- A remark: "Oh, wow, I've got my watch set to the wrong date!"
- An observation: "They got the whole street closed off down there."
- A sincere compliment: "I have to tell you, I just love your hat!"
- A request for an opinion: "I've never eaten here before. Is there anything you recommend?"

Start Small

If you're a naturally reserved person, make eye contact, smile, or say "hi" with someone you want to talk to. It's just a friendly thing to do. As a general rule, it's OK to make eye contact and/or smile at people who are around ten feet away. You can throw in a "hi" or "hello" to those within five feet of you. While standing or taking your place at a restaurant or sitting next to someone on a bus, you can make a comment about the location or something going on around: "Never got my umbrella when I need it," "Easy parking today." Even if it's just to yourself, people close by can hear you and some will react. Most people are friendly and perfectly open to chatting. It just takes a little push to cross the stranger barrier.

"I love this," Kim told me. "I absolutely hate the 'How's the weather' and 'How 'bout them Blue Jays eh' type of small talk. I make it a point to talk to most strangers like I do to my friends or family . . . if someone sneezes, I say 'bless you.' I compliment them on something cool they're wearing . . . some people think I'm crazy, but I usually get a very warm response. I've come to realize that if they are wearing it, they must like it, so how in the world would agreeing with them be stupid?"

Just Start Talking

The idea behind assuming rapport is that you don't use any particular opening line—you just start talking. As you learn to include details about whatever's going on around you at the time, you'll appear more casual and natural. It's not supposed to feel like a come-on or pickup. Casual is the key word. It's perfectly natural and friendly to exchange a few words with people in your daily comings and goings. This kind of friendly chitchat can happen in line at the supermarket, at a cocktail party, at a ballgame, on a plane, at an art gallery, at a business networking event—you name it.

Two years ago, Marketing Executive Lori Chambers attended a crowded networking event in Paris wearing a unique bracelet she had bought while teaching a Channel marketing workshop in Amsterdam. She decided to meet someone new by finding someone else with an interesting piece of jewelry.

"At the bar I bumped into a woman wearing a gorgeous silver and white bracelet. I complimented her on it, and she said, 'I was going to say the same thing to you.'" It turned out she headed a health tech company in the US. "Because I talked to a stranger, I landed one of the best connections of my career."

Emails like this confirm my faith in assuming rapport:

Hi, Nicholas. On a flight home from Washington DC last night, I discovered that the woman sitting beside me was on her way home from her husband's funeral out of state. It turns out her husband was a military veteran and had been ill before passing away. I was in the same situation just over a year ago—on my way home, alone, on a flight from my husband's out-of-state funeral. He had been ill and was a military veteran also. I had the opportunity to encourage her and share some important aspects of life I have learned over the past year. I gave her my contact information—inviting her for coffee or tea whenever she is ready. Thank you for challenging me to assume rapport and find common ground with strangers.

No-One Talks To Me Anymore

"One day at the grocery store I started speaking to an elderly man in front of me," Tarlan writes. "I made a comment about the lovely produce he was buying and he seemed surprised. When he was done checking-out, he turned to me with a tear in his eye and said, 'Thank you for talking to me. No one talks to me anymore. You're very kind.' I shed a tear thinking about it. It's so sad he has no one to talk to. This made one thing perfectly clear. We all need to talk to each other. We need to keep each other going."

Here Comes the Bride

"I made friends with someone on the train," says Rosie. "I ended up being a bridesmaid for her. Now I have a lovely group of friends locally. So, it's not hard. You just have to start a conversation."

Many of us go through life hoping that others will somehow read our minds and fulfill them without our having to say a word. Sometimes we're even disappointed or feel rejected when people don't provide what we want. The best way of getting what you want, though, is often just asking for it.

A Near Miss

Yesterday I flew from Munich to Detroit, wrote Christy. I so much wanted to take your advice and assume rapport with the woman sitting next to me just to see if I could, but she was playing a game on her phone, and the more I thought about it, the more I knew it wasn't going to happen. It just got further away from me until I stopped thinking about it.

When the plane touched down, we were both looking out the window and I was so disappointed in myself for being a coward that I just said to her, "I really like your ring," and she said, "I was thinking the same thing about the ring you're wearing."

In the time we taxied to the terminal, we talked non-stop, mostly about our jobs and exchanged cards.

Today I got this email:

Hi Christy. It was a pleasure to meet you yesterday. I just shared our conversation with my director on a team call. I'm going to be sending your contact info to him. He will be forwarding it to his key contact at our sister company. Your company could be a great fit for their portfolio.

Again, so nice to chat. I'm glad you initiated a conversation. I was engrossed in my silly word game on my phone just zoning.

Chapter 17:
You Call the Shots

Nobody can dictate what sparks joy, curiosity, or wonder in you. Nobody else can force you to see the world from a fresh perspective or to make connections between seemingly unrelated things.

You are the one who gets to choose how you spend your time, who you surround yourself with, and what you open yourself up to. You are the one who gets to decide whether to take the road less traveled, to ask the curious question, or to explore the uncharted territory.

If you are ready to unlock the power of Earth Angels and Magic Moments in your life don't wait for miracles to happen – create an environment where they can thrive.

Take the first step today! Here are seven simple yet

powerful actions to invite Earth Angels and Magic Moments into your life:

1. Turn Off The Blame Game

The blame game is a linguistic villain lurking in the shadows, ready to sabotage our lives. In a study called Blame Contagion, researchers Will M. Hart, John F. Dovidio and Samuel L. Gaertner determined that people who love pointing fingers and blaming others end up losing status, earning less and performing worse. It's like a self-destruct button they've unknowingly pressed. What's more, blame doesn't just mess with your success; it also snatches away your chances for positive change.

Blaming others is no big surprise. Listen to your friends, neighbors, and the media. We are surrounded by helpless language. "The politicians are to blame." "Blame it on the unions." "The doctor says it's impossible." "Life's too short." "It's Monday!" "Obesity is a disease." "He's shy." "It is what it is." "It's Friday—what do you expect?" "My ex is a complete jerk!"

Let it trigger an awareness in yourself to monitor your own thoughts and words until you can remove blame and excuses from your thinking.

2. Become A Temporary Optimist

When you approach life with optimism, you are more likely to notice patterns, make connections, and experience those magic moments, but hey, if you can't do that you can become a temporary optimist instead.

Here are some stats published by Time Magazine in late 2021.

- Optimists are 40% more likely than pessimists to get a job promotion in the next year.
- Pessimists report feeling stressed about money 145 days more than optimists in any given year.
- People with a positive style are 13% less likely to have a heart attack than those with a negative style.
- 80% of the human population is inherently optimistic.
- Optimistic men and women are more than 50% more likely to reach age 85 than their negative counterparts.
- Pessimists are five times more likely to get burned out than optimists.

- Optimists are six times more likely to be highly engaged at work than pessimists.

So, whistle and sing happy tunes to yourself for a few minutes every day and watch your life transform for the better.

- **Notice the small good things:** Instead of focusing on what's wrong, try to spot the little things that are okay or even good. Like a nice cup of tea or a friendly person.
- **Quick thanks:** Just take a second to think about a couple of things you're grateful for right now. Doesn't have to be a big deal.
- **Think about something nice coming up:** It could be later today or sometime soon, just something you're looking forward to.
- **Take a break from things that make you feel bad:** If the news or certain people are bringing you down, step away for a little while.

Being a temporary optimist is just about finding little ways to feel a bit better in the moment. You're not trying to be super happy all the time, just giving yourself a little boost when you need it.

3. Practice Non-Judgment

Judging events and circumstances is like applying the emergency brake while you're hurtling down a freeway. By learning non-judgment, we free ourselves up to pursue magic moments without restriction. My response to new people, events, and circumstances has always been "I wonder what this is all about?" or "Good luck, bad luck? Who knows?"

That said, while non-judgment promotes flow, avoiding judgment completely can cause problems. If we don't use some judgment, it's hard to figure out if something is harmful, or see when we need to judge a situation for practical, ethical, or safety reasons. Finding a balance is key. It means we can enjoy the good parts of being non-judgmental while still handling important situations wisely.

4. Release The Past

Before embarking on the next chapter, consider the power of forgiveness. Forgiveness liberates you from emotional burdens and enables you to see situations from different angles. Holding on to grudges and resentments only serves to slow flow.

Releasing the past does not mean erasing its existence or pretending it never happened. It's about relinquishing the grip of anger and resentment that have dragged you down for far too long and instead choosing to set foot on the path of progress.

Forgiveness, often seen as a sign of weakness, may, in fact, be one of the most formidable acts we can undertake. Consider this: what if forgiving someone is the key that unlocks our own liberation? What if, by pardoning the wrongdoings of others, we grant ourselves the freedom to forge ahead, unchained from the ghosts of the past?

Yet, let us acknowledge that there are certain wounds too deep to mend, certain transgressions that inflict irrevocable harm. In such instances, forgiveness may seem unattainable or require a significant passage of time. Additionally, some may struggle to forgive, unable to release the grip of anger and pain, or due to a perception that the wrongdoer fails to comprehend or accept the weight of their actions.

We all stumble at times, and we bear the weight of remorse for actions that haunt our conscience. Yet just as crucial is the act of forgiving ourselves. In granting forgiveness, we grant ourselves the liberty to do our own thing and embrace the untrodden path of our lives. For if we hold on to grudges and refuse to forgive, we shall forever remain prisoners of those who have wronged us.

5. Practice Mindfulness and Gratitude

One of the simplest ways to bring more Magic Moments into your life is to become more mindful of the present. By paying closer attention to the world around you, you're more likely to notice the small, beautiful moments that might otherwise pass you by. This can be as simple as appreciating a stunning sunset, a kind gesture from a stranger, or the sound of laughter.

Gratitude is another powerful tool. When you regularly practice gratitude, you train your brain to focus on the positive aspects of your life. This shift in focus can help you recognize and cherish Magic Moments when they occur, making them a more frequent part of your life.

6. Cultivate Kindness and Compassion

Earth Angels are often recognized for their kindness and compassion. To attract Earth Angels into your life, start by embodying those qualities yourself. Practice acts of kindness, whether it's helping a neighbor, volunteering, or simply being there for a friend in need. When you put kindness into the world, you naturally attract like-minded people—those who might be Earth Angels in disguise.

Being compassionate also means being open to others. Listen without judgment, offer help when you can, and be a source of support. This not only strengthens your relationships but also creates an environment where Magic Moments are more likely to occur.

7. Stay Open to New Experiences and Connections

Magic Moments often happen when you least expect them, especially when you're open to new experiences and meeting new people. Step out of your comfort zone—try a new hobby, travel to new places, or attend events where you can meet different people. Being open to the unknown increases the likelihood of encountering Earth Angels and experiencing Magic

Moments.

While the concepts of Earth Angels and Magic Moments are often framed in spiritual or mystical terms, there is scientific evidence that supports the underlying principles of how practicing mindfulness, gratitude, kindness, and fostering meaningful connections can positively impact our lives.

Mindfulness involves paying attention to the present moment without judgment. Studies have shown that practicing mindfulness can reduce stress, improve emotional regulation, and enhance overall well-being. According to research published in The Journal of Psychiatry Research, mindfulness practices have been linked to structural changes in the brain, particularly in areas associated with emotional regulation and empathy, which could explain why people who practice mindfulness are more likely to experience moments of joy and connection, akin to Magic Moments .

Gratitude is a practice that involves recognizing and appreciating the positive aspects of life. Research has shown that gratitude can improve mental health, increase life satisfaction, and strengthen relationships.

A study published in Personality and Individual Differences found that people who regularly practice gratitude report higher levels of well-being, happiness, and life satisfaction. This suggests that gratitude can make individuals more attuned to positive experiences, thereby increasing the likelihood of experiencing what might be described as Magic Moments

Acts of kindness boost happiness, not only in those who receive the kindness but also in those who give it. A study in the Journal of Social Psychology found that performing acts of kindness increases well-being and positive emotions. This can create a ripple effect, where both the giver and receiver experience moments of connection and joy, which can be seen as Magic Moments .

Compassion is linked to the release of oxytocin, often referred to as the "love hormone," which promotes bonding and reduces stress. Research published in the Journal of Clinical Psychology shows that practicing compassion and altruism can enhance mental health and lead to a greater sense of fulfillment. These benefits make it more likely for individuals to encounter Earth Angels—people who are naturally compassionate—and to experience meaningful interactions .

Strong social connections are one of the most significant predictors of happiness and longevity. A study by Harvard University, known as the Harvard Study of Adult Development, found that the quality of relationships is one of the most important factors in determining overall happiness and life satisfaction. Those with strong social ties are more likely to experience positive interactions and support, which can be interpreted as encounters with Earth Angels .

Research by Barbara Fredrickson, a leading psychologist in positive psychology, suggests that positive emotions broaden our awareness and encourage us to build new skills and resources. This "broaden-and-build" theory indicates that positive emotions, like those experienced during Magic Moments, can lead to increased resilience and well-being over time .

Optimism has been linked to better health outcomes, greater resilience, and higher levels of success. A study published in the Journal of

Personality and Social Psychology found that optimists are more likely to encounter positive experiences, as their mindset leads them to interpret situations more favorably and to persist in the face of challenges .

Letting go of rigid control and trusting in the flow of life can reduce anxiety and increase emotional well-being. Research published in *Psychological Science* suggests that individuals who are more flexible and accepting of life's uncertainties tend to experience lower stress levels and greater psychological resilience. This mindset can open individuals up to serendipitous moments and positive encounters .

Chapter 18:
The Hope Restorers

John's life was a digital haze, a never-ending blur of screens and swipes. He was a ghost in the machine, a loner content to spend his days lost in the virtual world. But on one fateful evening, in a crowded cafe in downtown Montreal, something sparked.

He noticed them first—an elderly couple, hands entwined, eyes aglow with a lifetime of love and laughter. They were a reminder that true connection wasn't about likes or shares, but about the warmth of a human touch.

John felt a pang of envy, a sting of regret. He realized that his digital life was a poor substitute for the real thing. This couple's love was a flame that burned bright, while his online connections were mere sparks, fleeting and superficial.

That moment was an epiphany, a wake-up call that shook John to his core. He knew he had to change, to trade his virtual life for a real one.

So, he started small. He put down his phone and struck up conversations with strangers. He joined an improv group, where laughter and creativity flowed freely. He volunteered at the local food bank, where the smell of fresh bread and the sound of warm voices enveloped him.

As John forged deeper connections with the people around him, he discovered a sense of joy and fulfillment he'd never known before. He found that real moments, emotions, and experiences were the keys to unlocking true happiness.

John's transformation was nothing short of remarkable. He went from being a digital ghost to a vibrant, living, breathing human being. And it all started with a single moment, a single connection that changed everything.

Months passed, and the transformation in John was

profound. Through his improv group, he discovered a knack for storytelling and public speaking and began hosting monthly storytelling nights at the hub, inviting locals to share their tales of resilience, love, and growth. His volunteer work at the food bank evolved into a thriving community initiative. He rallied local businesses to donate surplus food, transforming the food bank into a culinary learning center where people from diverse backgrounds gathered to cook, share recipes, and enjoy meals together.

If you think about it, the core purpose of life, since the dawn of time, has been to pass on what we've learned.

Strengthened Empathy and Compassion

Evicted from his apartment in San Francisco, Chris and his young son were forced to live in shelters and endure many hardships. His life changed completely one day when he saw a man parking a red Ferrari. Chris asked the man what he did for a living. He explained he was a stockbroker, and dots connected. Always fascinated by the stock market, but with no formal education or experience in finance, Chris had found his calling.

After developing and following a course of self education and attending investment seminars, Chris landed a job as an unpaid intern at a prestigious brokerage firm. His passion and purpose soon found him climbing the ranks and becoming a multimillionaire.

Years later, Chris Gardner's remarkable story captured the attention of Hollywood and was adapted into the critically acclaimed film "The Pursuit of Happyness," starring Will Smith as Chris.

Today, Chris is active in Peace Over Violence, a Los Angeles social-service agency working to prevent violence against women and children. "Giving back when you are successful should not be seen as an obligation; it's a privilege," he says, reminding us of our shared humanity and inspiring others to be more empathetic, compassionate, and engaged in making the world a kinder place for all.

A Sense of Purpose

Lily, a 35-year-old in Vancouver, grappled with mental health challenges and the weight of loneliness.

Determined to get out and get involved in the community, she turned to volunteering at a local animal shelter. Being around the animals and the volunteers, Lily unearthed a passion for animal welfare. Her experiences ignited a fire inside her, prompting her to establish a nonprofit committed to rescuing and finding homes for stray animals. As she dedicated herself to this project her journey from isolation to connection became a testament to the magic of reaching out.

A Catalyst

Meet Luna, a gentle soul with a warm smile and compassionate heart. Her presence is like a soft breeze on a summer day, carrying the sweet scent of possibility. With a listening ear and empathetic words, Luna helps revive the dreams that have lost their luster.

One day, while strolling through a quaint bookstore, Luna met Diana, a young writer whose creative flame had flickered out. Diana's passion for storytelling had been overshadowed by self-doubt and fear. Luna's guidance was like a ray of sunlight, illuminating the path to Diana's forgotten dreams.

With Luna's support, Diana began to nurture her writing again. Luna's encouragement was like a master gardener's tender care, helping Diana's creativity bloom. Together, they explored the world of words, and Diana's imagination was rekindled.

Luna's hope-restoring gift was not limited to Diana. She touched the lives of many, like a skilled artisan polishing precious gems. Her presence was a reminder that dreams are worth chasing, and that every setback is an opportunity to learn and grow.

As Luna shared her own stories of perseverance, her voice was like a soothing melody, calming the storms of doubt. Her laughter was contagious, infecting others with joy and positivity. In her company, the impossible seemed achievable, like a sunrise breaking through the horizon.

The Hope Restorer's impact was palpable, like the warmth of a crackling fire on a chilly evening. Luna's influence inspired others to become hope restorers themselves, creating a ripple effect of encouragement and support.

Diana's revived passion for writing was just the beginning. She started a blog, sharing her stories with the world. Luna's guidance had helped her find the courage to pursue her dreams, like a key unlocking a treasure chest.

As we encounter Hope Restorers like Luna, we're reminded that dreams are the spark that ignites our purpose. By embracing their guidance and support, we'll revive our passions, nurture our creativity, and make the impossible possible.

Luna's legacy was not measured by the number of dreams she revived, but by the hearts she touched and the lives she transformed. Her hope-restoring gift was a reminder that every dream deserves a chance to flourish, like a garden in full bloom.

"Just because someone tells you something can't be done, doesn't mean it's impossible," Luna shares with a knowing glint in her eye. "It just means they can't do it. It means they're limited by their own experiences, their own beliefs, and their own fears. But that doesn't mean you are. You have your own unique perspective, your own strengths, and your own determination. Don't let someone else's limitations define what you can achieve. Instead, use their doubts as fuel to push you forward, to innovate, and to find new solutions. Remember, the only way to truly know what's possible is to try, to experiment, and to explore.

Don't let anyone dull your sparkle or diminish your faith in the magic that lies within and around you.

Chapter 19:
Messages in the Making

Inside each of us there's a little spark. A tiny flame. It's what makes you, *you*. What gets you excited. Makes you dream big. For some, it's a cozy warmth, a quiet guide. For others? A full-on bonfire. A gotta-do-it feeling you can't ignore. This inner fire? It's where your best stuff comes from. It's the key to a life that means something. But so often? We forget it's even there. What if that burning inside is the very thing that can change everything? For you. Sure. But what if we're all born with a message tucked deep inside, something unique, something that could actually help mankind... evolve. Help the world go around.

What if finding it is the most important thing ever? What if we'd spare no expense to find it?

September 2011.

It was bucketing down as the shiny black Escalade slid out of terminal three at McCarran Airport. The driver leaned back.

"Straight to the hotel Mr. Boothman?"

"The Venetian. Yes." I texted my client. Landed. On my way.

The driver? Young. Maybe early twenties. Brown eyes. Symmetrical smile like out of a magazine. Super enthusiastic. Southern accent. Fit. Smart. Good posture. Waiting at baggage claim with my name on a tablet.

I was wiped. Oslo to Paris to Vegas. Long day. Head against the soft leather, I watched people grab their bags and disappear into the terminal.

"We had some crazy flooding over the weekend," the driver said, polite as could be.

Five-something in the evening. Sticky September air. Cruising down Paradise Road. Wife on speed dial. Landed okay. Motivational speaker rule number one? Get paid upfront. Good news. Rule number two? Missing a gig because of travel hell? Speaker nightmare. Bad news. That's why I always arrive early if I can.

"Heading straight back after your speech?" Driver's eyes in the rearview mirror.

"Next day. Don't do red-eyes anymore."

"'No red-eyes for Mr. Boothman.' Got it."

Sixth Vegas gig this year. No direct flights back to Toronto after two PM. Got to go through Atlanta or Dallas? Arriving home at nine AM? Done that. Never again.

We turned onto East Tropicana and the clouds broke. Sun peeked out. Rush hour traffic. We crawled along in silence.

"That's my dream," the driver said suddenly.

Snapped me awake. I leaned forward. "What do you mean?" I must've been dozing.

"Fame. Fortune. Hot hotels, first class flights, lounging in the back of a limo."

Slow right at the MGM Grand. Headed north on the Strip.

"I drive speakers around every day. Best restaurants, best hotels, TV shows."

Why burst the bubble? Fame and fortune? Maybe. Swanky hotels? Yep. Events happen there. First class? Not so much anymore. Unless you're a superstar.

"What do you think a motivational speaker does?" I asked. "Besides all the fancy stuff?"

Tourists everywhere. Grannies, kids, big guys, big girls, families. Shorts, shades, selfies. Vegas in full swing.

"Motivate people. Right? "

" … or inspire, or transform or challenge them." I added.

"Sorry. Am I bothering you?"

Eye contact in the mirror. "Would you do this job if you didn't get paid for it?" I asked.

"Probably not."

"Twenty-plus years speaking," I said. "Never met a truly great speaker who wasn't flat-out obsessed. With a purpose and a message burning inside them. Purpose first. Always expanding. Always wanting to connect. To help people get it. Yeah, the paycheck's nice. But that's not the fuel."

"Then what is it?" Relief in that question. Getting to the good stuff.

"To share a message. To plant a seed in those who need to hear it. Maybe even change something.

Silence hung in the air up front.

"So, what's your message? What do you burn to tell the world?"

Just then, two teenagers rushed to help an older couple who'd dropped their groceries. Small thing. But it hit me. That's it, right there.

"Do you have that?" I asked, my gaze sharp. "That purpose? That one unique thing inside you that could actually help make the whole damn world a little bit better?"

Silence.

"Got a message to share?"

Shrug.

"Got a unique story about your life?"

"Not really."

"Not famous? Didn't conquer some huge problem?"

"Nope."

"No rags-to-riches thing?"

Just a shake of the head.

"Didn't travel to some crazy place and come back with a secret formula?"

"No!"

"Pity. A unique story helps."

Silence.

"Don't worry. Your purpose is in there somewhere."

More Silence.

"And if it isn't?"

"Everyone has one. It's part of being human."

Michael Jackson's "Billie Jean" blasted from roadside speakers. Whoosh! Cheers! Bellagio fountains erupted. Six-thirty.

"What's your purpose?" Mature voice now. Presence. Gravitas. Maybe I misjudged the age.

Watching the fountains, listening to MJ, I felt lucky. Flashback to finding my own purpose. Walking one day. Asking myself, 'What have I *really* been doing my whole life?'

Picture in my head. Ten years old. School corridor. Teacher trying to explain fractions. Nobody got it. So I piped up, "Fractions are like pizza slices! Eight slices. You eat two? That's two-eighths, or one-quarter!" Teacher made me stand in the corridor. "Nicky Boothman! I told you not to do that!"

"I make complicated stuff sound simple and interesting," I said. "That's it. It's behind everything I do. Books, speeches. Easy to understand."

We turned onto the Venetian Bridge and stopped.

Gondoliers below. Fake lake. Candy-striped poles. Above? Fake Venice. Bell tower. Mosaic arches.

Reached into my bag. My book. Convince Them in 90 Seconds or Less. I offered it.

"Here. For you."

"Will you sign it?"

"Of course." I balanced the book on my knee.

"It's Julia, right?"

"Right." The driver turned.

"I'm Nick."

"Yes. I know." She smiled. "Mister Boothman. I Google all my rides."

I opened the cover and wrote: 'For Julia. Find your purpose. Free your spirit. Change the world.' Then I signed it.

Before I knew it, she was out of the Escalade, nudging the doorman. Insisted on taking my bags. Beaming. She threw up her hands. "How do I find my purpose?"

"What have you *really* been doing your whole life? What gives you deep joy? What makes you angry about the world? Your purpose is somewhere in between." I pressed the book into her hand.

"Sounds like a plan." Smile in her eyes.

"Julia, life doesn't care about your plans. Plans are fragile. Life's unpredictable. What matters? Your purpose. Why you're here. The difference you're meant to make. Find your purpose. Free your spirit. *Then* make your plans."

I turned and walked towards the crazy beauty of the Venetian's Palazzo Lobby.

This place is nuts.

I love my job.

Chapter 20:
Earth Angels in the Making

Eric Hogan sat in his kitchen, sipping coffee, working on his notes for his 10 o'clock interview with Woman's World Magazine and waiting for his toast to pop. The morning sun shone through the window, and just as he was about to open a fresh jar of peanut butter, his phone rang. He answered, hoping he hadn't messed up on his timing.

"Mr. Hogan?" a gruff voice asked.

"That's me." Eric replied.

"Mister Eric Hogan?" the voice repeated.

Eric's instincts kicked in. Something didn't feel right.

"I'm Daniella Lewis, vice principal at Lancaster County School," the voice continued.

As she spoke, Eric's toast suddenly caught fire. He

jumped up, burning his fingers as he grabbed the toast and tossed it in the sink.

"Shoot!"

"Yes, Mr. Hogan. Exactly."

"No. I wasn't referring to you. I just burnt my fingers."

"You certainly did," said vice-principal Lewis. "Am I right in thinking you collared some of our students in a local coffee shop recently? And interrogated them?"

"What are you talking about?"

"Selina, Anna, Lilly, Ben. Krispy Kreme. Ring a bell?"

"Come on!"

"Mister Hogan before we take this any further Principal Cox wants you to come to her office and explain yourself. Shall we say tomorrow morning at eleven?"

Why did that kind of voice make him feel ten years old and helpless all over again. He could feel his heart banging in his chest.

"I assume that wasn't a question?" Eric asked.

"Correct."

This is insane, Eric thought, sitting in the school office five minutes early. I'm 52 and I feel like I'm ten. I'm probably older than the Principal. Eric couldn't believe how his body was responding. He was actually alarmed.

"Mr. Hogan?" Eric stood up. "I'm Daniella Lewis, vice principal. "Everyone's ready for you now. Will you please follow me." She wore perfectly pressed, simple clothes and walked with a cane.

The Principal, a fair skinned woman with a combative look about her stepped out from behind a strikingly immaculate glass topped desk.

"Cassidy Cox." She held out her hand. "Thank you for coming Mr. Hogan."

She was short and slender with dark green eyes and thick dark brown hair with a messy fringe. Eric shook her hand.

"Ok?" Eric said.

Cassidy Cox carried on. "Let me introduce crisis worker Helen Lapierre, Regional Police Chief Eamon Larkin and my vice principal Daniella Lewis."

Eric nodded at them all and his bowels went weak.

"Can I sit down?"

Cassidy Cox indicated a seat.

"Daniella will you ask Selina and Ben to come in please."

This is it. Did I upload my files before I left. Thought Eric. I'm going straight to jail. I'm not going home.

The teens came in grinning. Ben said "Hi." Selina nodded. They sat next to Principal Cox.

"Well," said Cassidy Cox. "It seems like you left quite an impression on my students."

Eric shut his eyes, waiting for the coup de grâce. One quick shot to the temple should do it, he thought. Right here, dead on the principal's floor. Poetic justice. Just put me out of my misery.

He opened his eyes. They were all staring at him.

"The thing is Mr. Hogan," Principal Cox was frowning at him, "they want more."

Over the next six weeks Selina, Ben and vice-president Lewis came up with a plan for a public event called Speak-Up or Shut-Up? A local insurance broker offered to sponsor advertising to schools, parents and grandparents on radio, TV and social media and purchase 500 copies of one of Eric's books to give away to every audience member who stayed to the end.

A local coffee shop became the touch point for the five dollar tickets: the money to be split between the food bank and the women's shelter. The town offered a five hundred seat auditorium at the sports arena.

Crisis worker Helen Lapierre and Regional Police Chief Eamon Larkin from the Human Trafficking division spread the word to their contacts and women's shelter director Kitty Washington fired up her network.

For their part, Lancaster County School would provide the content. Two teams of three students each would have a maximum of ninety seconds each to present their case, with coaching from a freshly revived Eric Hogan. Then the audience would vote for Speak-Up or Shut-Up.

Simple. Effective. What could go wrong?

Chapter 21:
Help Me Find My Purpose

Check-in at The Venetian was smooth and friendly. The next morning? Two hundred and thirty engineers and salespeople. I got a standing O, signed a bunch of books, and answered questions. By 12:45, I'd shook hands and said bye to the client and her crew. On to the next thing for them.

The cleanup guys rolled in. I headed for the marble jungle of The Palazzo Lobby. Good habits taught me to check I'd left nothing behind. I dropped my shoulder bag onto a cruiser table by the door and took stock. All good.

Then she just walked in.

A young woman. Small string bag. Crisp white shirt. Short blue skirt. Purpose in her step. Dark hair in a ponytail. Freckles. Cute. She dropped the string bag. Soft thunk. No smile. No hello. Just those eyes.

Piercing. Direct.

"Julia?" I asked, my voice low. This whole thing felt off. Like a scene from a movie I'd accidentally walked into. "I don't believe this." I still had that after-speech buzz, the good kind. Now it was getting mixed with a serious dose of what-the-hell?

Then she spoke again.

"You're an expert at helping people. You're good at it." Her voice trembled, just a little. Sadness seemed to weigh her down. But if you looked close, real close? There was a tiny flicker. A spark of hope in all that mess.

"Is it possible," she said, her voice firm but laced with a hint of desperation, "that I can buy an hour of your time?" She glanced around the lobby, her eyes flicking towards an old couple nearby.

"I need some help right now," she said. Her hand slipped into the string bag, and she pulled out a plain white envelope. She pushed it towards me, her fingers hesitating for a moment before releasing it.

The envelope was thick, and I could tell it contained a serious amount of cash. My eyes met hers, and I raised an eyebrow.

"One thousand dollars. One hour." Her voice steady. Eyes begging. Tension in the air. Waiting.

I was surprised at her brashness. But not by her action. I'd heard stories. A guy I knew offered a top developer ten grand, all his savings and then some, just to shadow him for one day. And yes, you guessed it. At the end of the day he offered him a job and told him to keep his money saying that he wanted people with that kind of hunger and initiative on his team. This story has always stuck with me. The power of being bold.

Julia? The same thing. Willing to risk it all. To put herself out there. To get what she wanted. The boldness? It might raise eyebrows but it showed she had something else. Confidence. Drive. Sometimes that's all it takes to get noticed. To open doors.

"Help me find my purpose." She said. Low. Urgent. Simple. Sincere. She caught me off guard.

I was trying to think it through, put myself in her shoes. "There are no guarantees," I warned. "I've got to be straight with you.

Determination flickered for an instant behind her brown eyes, like a spark of defiance.

"I don't have long." She glanced nervously at a slim gold wristwatch on a well-worn crocodile strap. Patek Philippe. Thirty grand easy. And the way she wore it? Quiet class. Old money passed down. Not made overnight. What could she possibly need from me?

"I have a flight to catch."

"Yes. I know. Tomorrow." She blushed and looked away "I don't do red-eyes." She said in a pretty fair imitation of my English accent. She looked back at me. "And I don't forget things either." There was something curiously impressive about her willingness to go for what she wanted.

"You're really serious aren't you, Julia."

"I read your book from cover to cover last night."

I looked down at the envelope. Must be full of fifties folded over. She pushed it closer. I picked it up. She didn't even blink.

"Why are you doing this?"

She was suddenly grim-faced. "Two hundred and sixteen days ago I watched my father die." She was more factual than emotional. "First it was a cough, then a cold, then he couldn't breathe. It was like a rock fell on me. In twenty-two days I lost my father, the ranch I grew up on—and my dignity." She continued, her voice steady. "But I found out, even then, I had a choice. Let the rock crush me, or to use it to climb higher. I chose to climb. I picked myself up, moved here and started driving for a living. It's not what I planned, but it's taught me more about people, about never giving up than any book or any speech."

She paused. Took a breath. "Life's precious. Short. Crazy. You learn things. Even in the dark. Forgiveness. Love."

Julia's eyes locked onto mine, her gaze piercing. "That's what I've got, and that's what I want to share. The power of forgiving, the beauty of toughing it out. Of never giving up, no matter what."

I was about to say something but she held up her hand. She wasn't done.

"I grew up on a ranch. Me, my dad, three nasty stepbrothers—and my guardian angel."

I put the envelope back on the table. "Julia. I am so sorry, but I can't take this."

"Take it," she said, her eyes locked on mine. "I

didn't say I lost everything." With a hint of defiance, she raised her right arm, revealing the watch. "Antique. Dad left me his collection. Old watches from the 1900s." A sly smile spread across her face as she added, "My stepbrothers weren't happy, but hey, now I have time on my hands."

With a clattering of glasses, three hotel employees rolled up carts beside us. Two more arrived with tables on a dolly. There was a flurry of tablecloths and water jugs. A guy with a badge came over to move us on.

Julia thrust the money at me. There was no way I was going to take it. She flashed a huge smile at the man with the badge. "Viva Las Vegas," she said then aimed her smile at me. "Take the money. You're going to earn it."

On the far side of the hall, a line of sofas faced each other, separated by low glass tables. "Ok." I said. "How about 5:30 right over there?"

"Uh-uh." She waved it off impatiently. "I'll pick you up outside the front door. Two hours."

Chapter 22:
The Great Debate

The lights dimmed, and the anticipation was palpable. The big night had finally arrived, and Cassidy Cox, the principal, took the stage with confidence and poise. "Welcome, everyone," she began, her voice echoing through the auditorium. "Tonight, six students will present their arguments on the age-old question: to talk to strangers or not to talk to strangers?"

The audience murmured, and the students took their seats on stage, their faces set with determination. Cassidy Cox introduced them one by one, and they stood up, smiling nervously. Eric Hogan, the guest speaker, took his seat at the end of the row, his eyes scanning the audience.

Cassidy Cox returned to the podium, surveying the

crowd with a keen eye. "We want you to decide, when you leave here tonight, do we speak up or shut up when it comes to meeting strangers?" she asked, her voice dripping with intrigue.

The audience was on the edge of their seats, eager to hear the arguments. Cassidy Cox smiled, a mischievous glint in her eye. "Our students have been challenged to make a convincing case in under two minutes. Three presenters will argue in favor of speaking up and talking to strangers – the Speak-Ups. And three presenters will argue against talking to strangers – the Shut-Ups."

The audience erupted into applause, and the debate began.

"Ladies and gentlemen, students, and esteemed guests, please join me in welcoming our first presenter, Benny Harris, who will bravely delve into the vulnerable topic of 'Baring Your Soul to a Stranger.' Benny, take the stage!"

Benny Harris, dressed to impress in his black jeans, burgundy tee, and bright blue Vans, stepped up to the microphone. His short stature and pale skin made him almost blend into the background, but his bright blue eyes shone with determination. Despite his visible nervousness, he began with a confident "Thank you."

As he placed his cue cards and water bottle on the podium, his hands trembled slightly. The audience, comprised of local students, business owners, city workers, truck drivers, and members of the police department, watched with anticipation. The majority of the crowd was female, and their supportive gaze seemed to steady Benny's nerves.

Behind the scenes, Kayleigh Chen, clad in sleek black attire, expertly managed the technical aspects. She controlled the sound system and timing, using a giant red and black gym timer to keep the speeches on track. As Benny tapped the microphone, Kayleigh jumped, adjusting the volume in her headphones before starting the timer and angling it toward the podium.

Eric winced. Oh no. He knew what was coming next. Sure enough the water bottle rolled off the sloping top of the podium and on to the floor at Ben's feet.

Ben thought for a second, then disappeared and reappeared holding the bottle among muffled giggles and sneers. Kayleigh restarted the timer.

"Honestly, have you ever noticed how it's way easier to spill your guts to someone you don't even know? Like, you'll tell some random guy at the gym or a taxi driver or even the lady who needs her driveway shoveled, but you won't tell your own family or friends?

"I mean, think about it.

"First, there's no drama. They don't know all the weird stuff about you, like how you always blame others for your problems or how much you hate your stepdad. They only know what you tell 'em.

"Second, you get a fresh perspective. Your friends and family are sick of hearing you complain about the same stuff over and over, but a stranger might actually have some useful advice.

"And, third, some scientist at UBC, Dr. Elizabeth Dunn, found out that talking to a stranger can actually make you happier than talking to a friend! Who knew?

"So yeah, let's all just Speak-Up and be happy,

right? Thanks for listening, I guess."

Kayleigh tapped the timer. A man in the fourth row got to his feet and started clapping very loud. Half a dozen people around him got up and joined in. Soon the whole place was up applauding Ben.

Principal Cox stepped back to the podium clapping, smiling and proud.

Ben grinned at the man in the fourth row who started the ovation. It was his gym teacher Mr. Dodd. Ben went back to his seat.

"And now, representing the Shut Up side, please welcome Naomi Parkes."

A thin, serious girl in a loose-fitting dark green dress with sunken grey eyes and shoulder-length hair drifted up to the podium. She began slowly, pausing between each sentence—without notes.

"My friend Lauren's sister got trafficked when she was literally my age. She thought she knew what to expect, like she'd get kidnapped and locked in a basement or something. But nope. It started with some dude on Insta who was all sweet and stuff. He was like, two years older and made her feel special. He'd send her money and gifts, and she thought he was her boyfriend or whatever.

"But then, he started asking for help with some "problem" he had, and said if she didn't help, he'd post some private pics of her online. She was totally trapped. And the worst part is, she didn't even know how to protect herself. She didn't have many friends, and this guy just pulled her away from her family.

Naomi's voice trembled as she scanned the room, her eyes welling up with tears and frustration. "I thought I was going to talk about shut up for us students when they start chasing us online, but it's not, is it?"

She moved to the front of the stage and began to single out the adults.

"It's about speaking up to you. And you, and you. You guys, you're the adults, like, it's your job to keep us safe! It's not just about giving us food and a place to sleep, okay? We need to know how to protect ourselves from all the crazy stuff that's out there. If you can't even teach us that, then what's the point? I'm sorry, but it's true. We need to know how to protect ourselves, 'cause this can happen to anyone. Literally, anyone. So, speak up for us. Yeah?"

Naomi turned and headed back to her seat in silence. Then she changed her mind, raised her arms, and said, "Sorry. Thanks." Then she walked down the steps at the side of the stage.

Crisis worker Helen Lapierre shuffled after her.

Regretting the whole event Cassidy Cox returned to the podium.

"I am so sorry," she said fanning herself with her notes, "This is not what we had in mind."

Ben got up and came to Cassidy's side. "No." Ben said into the mike. "That was solid gold. Yes? Yes?"

Mr. Dodd once again sparked a round of applause, and the audience eagerly joined in, rising to their feet in a standing ovation. The enthusiasm gradually subsided, allowing Principal Cox to continue.

"With that impressive display behind us, let's move on to a lighter note," Principal Cox said with a smile. "Please welcome Sophie Mendoza for the Speak-Ups!"

Mr. Dodd started clapping and the audience joined

in and slowly got to their feet. Ben returned to his seat.

"Oh yes," said Principal Cox talking over them, "and delivered in two minutes and twenty four seconds."

The applause subsided.

"Now on a lighter note," said principal Cox, "Sophie Mendoza for the Speak-Ups."

A short girl with narrow shoulders, long arms, a narrow torso, straight hips, and short legs trundled up to the podium. It was obvious she'd been moved to tears by Naomi's plea.

She put down her notes and blew her nose – right into the microphone.

"Oh whoops," she said and Naomi's spell was broken. So were Kayleigh's eardrums.

"Hey guys, let's think about this... what's more creative, hanging out with the same old friends or meeting new people?

"I mean, imagine putting together a bunch of totally different strangers - like, a barista, a firefighter, a ballerina, a baseball player, a rapper, a casino dealer, and even someone who's been to jail!

"When we talk to people who aren't like us, we can break out of our routines and see things in a whole new way.

"You could learn a new language, join a band, become a chef, fix a lawn mower (lol), write a book, or make new friends. There's literally someone out there who can help you with whatever you want to do, as long as you're brave enough to speak up!

"And let's be real, our friends were all strangers once too... until we started talking to them! So, the more people you meet and talk to, the faster you'll make new friends and have new experiences. It's pretty simple, but it's true! Thanks for listening! Oh yes, so speak up."

The audience was politely clapping when Naomi wafted up the side steps behind Sophie and took her seat next to Ben. The polite clapping turned into thunder. Sophie was beaming by the time Principal Cox came up to shuffle her off back to her place.

"Thank you Sophie. Well, we're at the halfway point and I'd like to say a couple of things."

She pretended not to read from notes.

"Giving a stranger a small smile or even just making friendly eye contact as you pass can have a big impact on their feelings and their health. Even the smallest amount of eye contact, or a smile, or both, can make people feel connected to others. But your body-language can also be used to hurt people, sneering, jeering, leering, pointing. Not good."

"Anyway now I'd like to introduce Pargash Reid for the Shut-ups."

A thin boy with shoulder-length black hair, tight black jeans and a flowing white shirt marched up to the mike.

"Hi. Honestly, what's the big deal about grabbin' a coffee by myself? I'm an introvert, and when I finally get some alone time, it's like, my happy place, you know? So, just leave me be and don't bother me, eh? I've got friends and all, but I'm good doin' my own thing. I don't get lonely or anything, and I'm not really into chatting with random strangers in public, unless it's like, a quick hello or something.

"I'm all about tech, and I love my alone time. Sometimes I'll whip out my phone to escape the chaos in busy areas, but it's weird, right? Everyone's always stuck to their screens, ignoring their kids or the people around 'em. It's like, we've got all this communication, but we're still super lonely, you feel me?

"So yeah, just let me be, and don't bug me, okay?"

With that Pargash's mouth twitched and he burst into a genuinely sweet white smile. He looked into the audience and said, "Thanks eh. And like shut up—kind of."

Cassidy Cox was back at the mike with more goodies.

"Thank you very much, Pargash."

Pargash returned to his seat and Principal Cox waited for the room to come to order.

"In the Alameda County Study from the Harvard School of Health Sciences," she began, "Dr. Lisa Berkman and her team carefully looked at 7,000 people, aged 35 to 65, over a period of nine years."

She was losing her audience.

"Wait you'll find this very interesting."

The room hushed slightly.

"Their study concluded that people who actively

socialize and meet new people are almost three times less to die of medical illness than those who don't." She folded her notes. "I thought you might like to know that. Just for the record."

"And now Anwar Malik to talk about loneliness."

A short boy in a grubby corduroy cap, a checkered shirt and baggy jeans that had seen better days, waddled over to the center of the stage with his hands in his pockets.

He turned to the row of presenters at the back of the stage. "Pargash man; nobody actually wants to be lonely."

"Wait, wait." Kayleigh Chen sprang from the side of the stage like Catwoman carrying a cordless microphone. She jammed it in Anwar's left hand and disappeared. Anwar turned to the audience.

"Nobody wants to be lonely. We all need someone to talk to, someone who gets us, someone who'll listen and tell us how it is—even if it's tough love sometimes. We need someone to tell us we're not alone, and that they're there for us."

Anwar's voice cracked as he spoke, his eyes

scanning the audience with empathy.

"Loneliness is real, guys. It's everywhere - in our schools, our places where we worship, on the streets. It doesn't matter how old you are, where you're from, or what you look like. That feeling that can hit anyone."

He fidgeted with a piece of paper, his hands shaking slightly.

"The stats are crazy - 32% of people have never even met their neighbors, and 27% feel like nobody understands them. And the worst part is, our generation is the loneliest one yet."

Anwar's voice broke as he spoke, his hand on his heart.

"We can't just ignore the pain and helplessness that's making us OD and stuff. We need to talk about it, we need to listen to each other."

The sad little figure at the center of the stage pleaded to the audience.

"Speak up if you're lonely."

He bit his lips together and waited.

"Like my sister Fatima…" Anwar tried in vain to bring his emotions under control.

"Speak up if you want to. My name is Anwar. And I'll listen to you."

The room was riveted. Even Regional Police Chief Eamon Larkin sitting in the second row had his Kleenex out pretending to clean his glasses. Time stood still for a few moments. Then Catwoman ran on stage, took the mike from Anwar's hand and hugged him.

Anwar returned to his seat going out of his way to high five Pargash on the way.

Cassidy Cox was back at the podium. "Jesus. I never expected this," she said to herself realizing all too late the podium mike was right in front of her picking up her every word. She reached out to cover it with her hand, but not in time to stop her next gem being broadcast. "Oh crap." Which was immediately followed by a piercing squeal of feedback as her hand covered the mike. At least the audience didn't hear her round it off with "buggar."

Students erupted in giggles, half the adults closed their eyes and the rest bounced merrily in their seats.

"Oh dear," said the Principal, "right. Thank you Anwar for your heartfelt appeal. And now our final student today is Selina Malik to convince us all about stranger danger."

Principal Cox turned to the row of presenters and waved Selina up to the microphone. She wore a white shirt, a denim miniskirt and black Doc Martins. Instead of heading for the podium she took off in the direction of Catwoman. "Hey. Can I have that?"

Thrilled, Catwoman launched herself onto the stage and presented the mike to Selina with a bow followed by a theatrical ta-daa to the audience and a covert finger-wave to Anwar.

"I am very, very confused." Selina began.

She walked to the front of the stage and addressed a couple of thirty-something guys in the third row.

"I bet you never had to walk down the street and there's a group of boys or a man and you have to cross the street to avoid them. Huh?"

She moved along to two young women sitting together.

"We all do it don't we? As a human person I have to go out of my way because of another person, another human person. It's not their fault, I don't know them, they could be my future best friend for all I know but everyone tells me I'm supposed to be frightened of strangers. That's not fair."

"Ever since we've been kids," Selina continued, "our parents have drilled 'strangers are dangerous' into our heads. They're not wrong. As a girl, who is always told be careful when in public, I have to mind what I say or do with everyone. If I decide to nod or smile at someone on the street, I have to think about the consequences first. What if my smile or speaking to a random person leads them on to thinking I'm interested in them and then they become a stalker?"

Selina closed her eyes, held her breath and froze for a few seconds. Then exhaled and opened her eyes.

"But, every now and then, one of them smiles or says something and it really perks me up. It's a really small gesture but it's magical in making me feel better."

"Speak up? Shut up? I don't know anymore."

Lots of nods from the audience. Then applause. Cassidy Cox was up again.

"Well, yes ladies, gentlemen and students isn't that

the truth. Thank you Selina, that's the question we're all here to answer this evening. A big round of applause please, and thanks to Mr. Hogan who showed them how to do it. An invaluable skill."

"And now the man himself."

Eric came to the podium amid polite applause. "Thank you."

Catwoman had been warned Eric wanted a cordless mike and she was ready. She pranced across the stage and placed it in Eric's outstretched hand then departed like a flatfooted black swan from Swan Lake.

"Hi everyone, thanks for coming."

"You know the secret of success in life isn't very hard to figure out. The better you are at connecting with all kinds of different people the more success you're going to have. I think these six students did an incredible job of connecting with a lot of complete strangers here this evening.

Chapter 23:
An Unexpected Departure

The Vegas sun hammered the back of my neck as I stood on that fake Venetian bridge. Three o'clock hit. Right on the nose. The black Escalade sliced through the crowd. Smoked windows. Couldn't see a thing inside. Then the door opened. An old guy in white overalls got out. Looked like he'd wandered off a construction site. But his smile was warm and real. He headed straight for me.

"Mister Nick?" he spoke softly with a trace of an accent.

I nodded.

"Mannie Esposito, I'm from Julia."

"Oh yes?" He saw the question mark on my face.

"She's waiting for me to bring you."

Around us the bells of the Basilica. The warbling

vibrato of "The Gondolier March" drifting up from the canals.

"Hey Jules – I got him." I hadn't seen the yellow Motorola two-way in his hand until he lifted it to his mouth. He let go the talk button.

Her voice came through the tiny speaker. "Mister Boothman, this is Mannie. He's my," she paused. Shouting now. Something was flapping in the background. "He's my... boss."

"What's going on Julia? Where are you?"

"I got a surprise for you. Five minutes away. Please. Mannie will bring you."

The Venetian to Circus Circus Not even a mile and a half. Mannie mumbled into that Motorola twice, but the words? We peeled left off the Strip then north on Sammy Davis Junior Drive and into the back of Circus Circus right into the Adventure Dome parking lot. And wouldn't you know it? Right on cue, a blue and white Robinson helicopter – SkyValley Tours painted on the side – touched down maybe fifty feet away.

Mannie scooted around the limo, yanked my door open like he was pulling a grenade pin. No words. Just a hard stare and a wave. Towards the chopper. I didn't budge. He cupped his hands. Yelled over the idling engine, "Go. Now!"

This whole thing felt wrong. But something in Julia's voice on that crackly radio. Something in Mannie's eyes, despite the hard edge. Made me suck in a breath. Stepped forward.

Chopper door swung open. Dark-haired woman in a purple skirt, white blouse. Holding onto the frame like it might fly away without her. Waved me over. Hurry up. I saw another woman inside. Younger. At the controls. Talking into a headset. Julia?

Tourists were stopping. Pointing. Helicopters in Vegas are a big deal. But still… the whirring blades. The mystery. Got people staring. Thinking about money. Power. The kind of stuff that stays in your dreams.

"Go go go!" Mannie again. Louder now. Blades chopping the air.

"Not a chance in hell!" I yelled back. Point-blank.

"Because she's a woman?" His eyes narrowed.

"Hell no. Because I don't know any of you!"

"Know this then. Julia? More than two thousand hours flying these things."

Mannie jammed the Motorola to his mouth. "He's not going."

Julia looked over at me. Raised both hands. Like saying, *What can I do?*

Mannie's hand clamped on my shoulder. Pulled me close. Mouth by my ear. "Do what feels right. Three seconds."

He looked away. Waited. Then, into the radio. "Shut her down, Jules. We swap places." He turned to me. "She drive you back in the limo. You do your thing there. Big pity. She had a very nice plan."

"Damn it." Should have known better. "Okay. I'm going."

I duck-walked to the open door. The woman grabbed my arm and helped me in then slammed the door shut. Then she was gone, ducking low towards Mannie.

Julia whipped a headset off the passenger seat – right before my butt landed on it – and shoved it at me.

"Where are you taking me?"

"Buckle up. Not far." She yelled above the thwuping of the blades. I adjusted the four-way harness and fumbled the headset into place. The mechanical sounds faded into the background.

"McCarran Tower, helicopter Zero-Mike-Tango, request VFR departure out of Circus helipad to the east not above fifteen hundred, heading south leaving your area." It took me a moment to realize the voice in the headset really was Julia's.

The reply came back fast. "Helicopter Zero-Mike-Tango, McCarran Tower, clear for takeoff, report one mile east at or below two thousand."

She confirmed the tower's instructions then jabbed me with her elbow and smiled. "Give me a minute."

With a smooth gentle touch she had us crabbing up and away from the helipad, over the Las Vegas Strip and east toward the Hoover Dam.

She was talking to the tower and methodically scanning the sky around us.

Fifteen minutes ago I was on the ground at The Venetian, now I'm a thousand feet in the air above it and halfway to the Hoover Dam.

She flicked us to intercom. "Give me a sec to get us out of here. Tower says there are over eighty aircraft in his control zone. I can only see four of them."

Shoot. I couldn't see any. No point protesting now. I shut up and let her get on with it.

Two minutes later we turned right and headed south. Five minutes after that we set down in the parking lot across from what looked like a cowboy set from a wild west movie. The sign over the general store on the main street read Eldorado Canyon Mine.

I pulled off my headset.

"What the hell are we doing here?"

Julia ignored me and finished her shut down procedure.

"Didn't expect this did you?" She said flicking three switches in quick succession. "You said finding your gift is like looking for gold right? What better place to look for gold than right here. This was the oldest, richest and most famous gold mine in Southern Nevada. Now it's a tourist trap."

With that, she pushed open her door, came around to my side and let me out.

"I booked a space out back on the patio where we can talk in private."

"Who's paying for this?" I said slapping the

helicopter door.

"No-one," she said as she walked backwards in front of me, a red backpack slung over her left shoulder. "It's mine."

"On a limo driver's pay!"

Coolly she flexed her fingers and stopped in her tracks. I nearly walked into her.

"You can spot more stray cattle in an hour in that than you can in a week on horseback."

"Big ranch?"

"Big enough. Mannie ran the place. You don't mess with an ex-mercenary from Mozambique. He's hard as nails and utterly ruthless when he has to be." She screwed up her eyes for a second. "Kept my stepbrothers in line—until my dad died."

We paused outside the general store. The half dozen tourists who'd rushed out to see the helicopter arrive drifted back to the store muttering about us.

"Wait here." She disappeared behind a mound of rusty cartwheels, tumbleweed and pumpkins, each one with a price tag attached, and into the store.

After the helicopter ride it was quiet here. Peaceful.

I laughed.

Julia was back. "Come."

"Is that the end of the story?"

"Mannie taught me to fly choppers I was sixteen."

She led me around the back of the dusty store. It opened onto a small clearing with a barbecue pit made of red brick, a couple of homemade picnic tables, and half a dozen homemade chairs. Even an old-fashioned water tower like you'd see in a black and white movie.

Dark clouds were gathering over the mountains. Last weekend's flash floods flashed through my mind..

Julia dropped her knapsack on to a picnic table.

"You okay with this?" She asked, her eye steady.

"Sure." I pushed the whole pilot thing to the back of my mind. I reached inside my jacket, pulled out my well-worn thesaurus, and laid it on the table, respectfully, followed by a stack of folded paper, and a couple of pens. I looked again at the dark clouds. "

"Hey. Let's get started."

Chapter 24: The Verdict

Eric stood before the audience, his presence commanding attention. The debate had been fierce, the arguments passionate. But as he began to speak, it was clear that he had a verdict to deliver.

"Let's face it," he said, his voice firm and resolute. "The world is a complex and often scary place. But by teaching our kids to shut up and avoid strangers, we're not keeping them safe – we're crippling them."

He paused, scanning the crowd. "We're raising a generation of kids who are afraid to take risks, afraid to ask questions, and afraid to connect with others. And that's a recipe for disaster. So, I want to round the evening off by talking about the power of chance encounters. We've all been taught to be cautious around strangers, and rightfully so. Our personal safety is important, and we should always prioritize it. But I believe that with some basic precautions and an open mind, talking to strangers can lead to life-changing experiences, new friendships, and unexpected opportunities.

"But let's be clear: safety always comes first. When engaging with strangers, trust your instincts, meet in public places, and tell a friend or family member where you'll be and who you'll be with. Don't feel pressured to share personal information or go anywhere that makes you uncomfortable.

"By taking these basic precautions, we can minimize risks and maximize the benefits of chance encounters. We can build connections, foster community, and grow as individuals. So, I want to leave you with a challenge today. Next time you're in a public place, take a chance and strike up a conversation with a stranger. You never know where it might lead. Just remember to prioritize your safety, be aware of your surroundings, and trust your instincts. Let's build connections, let's build community, and let's see the world in a new light because we can't live without each other. Literally!"

"We need the emotional input of other humans as much as we do the air we breathe and the food we eat. Deprive us of it and we will wither and die just as surely as if we were deprived of food and fresh air."

"But, when strangers come together, joy and knowledge can be shared, love and hope can be found, food can be grown, diseases can be cured, the environment can be saved and miracles can happen every day, every hour, every minute: because the biggest miracle of all—is you.

"So speak up and make someone's day. It might just be your own. Thank you."

Silence. The calm before the storm. Eric was used to this response. Stuff still sinking in. Then the audience rose as one. A full standing ovation.

Catwoman was up and prowling across the stage to get the mike with both hands on her heart. As she approached Eric Hogan she the opened her arms wide and was closing her hands around the mike when Cassidy Cox plucked it out of Eric's hand.

Heck for a minute there I thought she was going to hug him too, thought Principal Cox still entranced with the notion of her pupils being little miracles.

Catwoman blushed and for a moment and didn't know what to do. "It's ok," Eric said, "stay here next to me." He turned and called the other presenters to join him and the place went nuts. After a minute Principal Cox signaled to the standing audience she had something to say.

"Please, stay standing." The place went quiet.

"What just happened here tonight?" She asked the room. I'll tell you. A bunch of strangers came together and made magic. That's what happened. So here's what you can take away from tonight. Your voice matters and your story deserves to be heard. When you speak up you can uplift and inspire others. And by speaking up, you create space for magic to unfold."

Another round of applause.

"All those in favor of speaking up."

Chapter 25:
A Purpose Quest

We sat facing each other. The shade felt good. It was dead quiet. Not even a whisper of wind.

My hands moved on their own. Smoothing out the folded papers. Lining up the thesaurus and the pens. Neat. Then I took one sheet. Folded it long ways.

"Close your eyes," I said, my voice low. "Just… relax."

Julia unwrapped her sweater. Slow. Deliberate. Folded it over her backpack. Placed them on the bench beside her. Rested her hands on the rough wood of the table and closed her eyes. "Okay."

"This starts with something I call the Parable of Purpose. It goes like this…"

"Imagine, in your mind's eye, that a few moments before you are born, you find yourself in a line-up with a slip of paper in your hand. On that paper, you have to write, in one short phrase, the reason you deserve to be born. The only condition is that it has to be something of benefit to humanity, because we know humanity evolves over time. Let's call this your Purpose Statement.

"This scenario obviously isn't real. It's a parable, a made-up tale told to teach a lesson or share a moral message, so it's easy to remember and relate to.

"When you get to the front of the line, the powers-that-be look at your slip of paper and either say, "Not good enough; go back and try again," or else they say, "Great, very good; you can get born."

"Armed with your Purpose Statement they send you over to the "To-Be-Born Supply Department" to be fitted out with all the attributes and talents you'll need to accomplish your purpose.

"Depending on what you've written, they might grant you patience, caring, courage, humor, organizational skills, eloquence, a flair for languages, drawing or music, etc.—whatever you'll need.

"Once you are filled to the brim with your attributes and talents, you are ready to be born. But here's the catch: just before you leave, the powers-that-be tear up your slip of paper and wipe your conscious memory.

"And so you enter the world with an unshakeable sense that you were meant for more. You may find yourself drawn to certain professions, or certain causes, without quite knowing why. You may have a talent or a skill that seems to come naturally, without any formal training. All the while, that sense of purpose burns within you, driving you ever forward, even as you struggle to understand what it all means.

"So, here you are, knowing deep down that you are uniquely equipped for something, but you haven't a clue what it is. Not consciously.

"By the time we leave this place, you'll know what was on that slip of paper. Your Purpose Statement. And with that? Things change. A path starts to appear. You begin to see that life? It's not just happening *to* you. It's happening *for* you.

"So, give me seven words to describe you."

Chapter 26: Purpose Statements

We've talked a lot about how Earth Angels and Magic Moments touch our lives. Knowing what you're here for, your purpose, helps you see those things even more clearly. When you're tuned into how you can help the world go around, you start noticing the people who are genuinely trying to help and those little moments that feel like a wink from the universe. It's like your purpose acts as a kind of magnet, helping you pick up on all the good signals that are already out there.

Did you ever ask someone, "Tell me about yourself," and watch their eyes glaze over? You can't blame them. They don't really know. They've been labeled since day one by other people. "You're so clever." "You're shy." "Why are you so clumsy?" Trying to find your purpose built on someone else's idea of who you are? It's the fast train to nowhere. You've got to dig deeper. Way deeper.

Ask someone to give you seven words to describe themselves and you'll soon discover they can't: not accurately. For example, they might say they are "caring", "creative" and "organized" when, if you dig a little deeper, you discover that when they say caring, what they actually mean is "vigilant." When they say "creative" when what they really mean is "inventive." And by "organized" they may really mean "methodical".

This may seem like splitting hairs but a caring, creative, organized person is not the same person as a vigilant, inventive, methodical person. This becomes more obvious when you look at the negative words people use to describe themselves. Words like "I am 'shy'," "I'm 'negative'," "I am 'antisocial'." You weren't born that way. If someone believes these descriptions of themselves just imagine the catastrophic consequences of decisions made based on these beliefs. How can anyone make a fresh start if they don't know who they are to begin with?

The truth is there's no such thing as a negative

attribute: only positive ones turned upside down by time and circumstance. Jackson told me he was shy. His mother called him shy when he was growing up. "Oh yes Jackson's such a shy boy." "Oh Jackson. Stop being so shy!" Well jeepers. Hearing this over and over, the seeds are sown. When Jackson discovers there's no such thing as shy—that it's not a natural-born attribute—and that he's actually "cautious and reserved," which are good things, his negative self-esteem stops holding him back and he's able to move along a different, stronger path.

"People say I'm negative" Mehdi explained, "I'll be in a meeting and someone comes up with a great idea and I get mad that I didn't come up with an idea like that myself." I pointed out that he was probably defining "competitive" not "negative". He was relieved to get closer to his true self.

In March 2001 a Canadian organization called WRED, Women and Rural Economic Development, contacted me to produce a program to reveal hidden strengths in women. My team and I had spent three years developing a project designed to cast-off constraining beliefs and reveal liberating natural-born strengths in men and women. We called the project Purpose Quest.

Although the techniques were developed for all types of people, WRED aimed their program at women living in particularly belligerent surroundings (though men could attend if they wanted). Many of the their lives were changed immediately.

A troubled woman in her late thirties, Susan attended one of these workshops. She lived on her husband's family farm thirty miles north of Toronto. It was her duty to cook, clean, shop and wait on her in-laws: mother, father, brother and uncle as well as help them out around the farm when things got hectic.

Susan was at her wits end: insecure, depressed and anxious. We began by telling her it's okay to not feel okay. That it really helps to allow yourself to feel whatever emotions are coming up. "Everywhere I turn, I'm marooned," she said. "I don't know whether to go forward, backward. left right. I don't know which way to turn."

When asked to come up with seven words to

describe herself she snapped, "I'm an aggressive, angry bitch for starters: or so I'm told." She eventually added: methodical, loyal, challenging and impatient.

An hour later we'd accurately reframed the words she gave me to describe herself. When we dug deep down 'aggressive' became 'stimulating,' 'angry' became 'quick-witted,' 'bitch' turned into 'having high standards' and 'impatient' changed to 'ambitious.' The rest stayed the same.

In a flash Susan realized how over the years the people around her had poisoned her self-talk, turned her strengths into weaknesses and had her believing all these negative things about herself. No wonder a stimulating, quick-witted woman with high standards, living in the circumstances she did, was told over and over she was an aggressive, angry bitch. Sooner or later we start to believe what people say. But Susan's lights went on that day as we peeled back the layers and discovered what she'd always been great at since she was a child. What made her deep-down angry about society in general and what gave her great joy.

"This is it," Susan said as her truths revealed themselves and the words came to her, "This is what I do. I can't help it. This is me."

Six years later I was giving a keynote speech at The International Plaza Convention Center in Toronto. I'd just got off the escalator when someone called my name.

"Hey Nick."

I turned.

"You don't remember me do you?"

The woman looked familiar. "Help me out," I said.

"It's me. Susan."

We hugged. "You look amazing," I said. "What are you doing here?"

"I manage three teams at the Ministry of Agriculture and they're running public focus groups here today. I'm wandering from room to room keeping an eye on them."

Susan was laughing. "It's been incredible," she said. "When I recognized that I was the only person who could change my life I became incredibly focused and confident and, believe it or not, I started talking to strangers. That was magic. Really scary for the first couple of times but then it was like finding Christmas presents all over the place and opening them. It got me out of the house and into a job with a title: Field Information Officer. We analyze soil samples to optimize plant growth."

"My Purpose Statement pointed me in the right direction and from that moment on I just needed to ask myself, 'am doing it now or not?' If I was doing it, there was joy and opportunities appeared and doors opened and I acted on them. It was almost scary at first. If I wasn't doing it I'd drift off track.

Susan's Purpose Statement? "I challenge people to imagine wild, new ideas."

Purpose Statements seem trite and puny to other people, but they are totally inspirational to the person who's statement it is. It's as if suddenly there's a point to their life, a direction to their reason for being and unity to their enthusiasm. But, to anyone else they don't mean much.

Here are a few examples.

"I challenge people to imagine wild, new ideas"

"I make people away from home feel like friends"

"I search out and bring art to the world"

"I challenge the status quo and design products that are beautiful and user friendly"

"We change the world through stories"

"I seek patterns of order so I can protect others"

"I give women the courage to succeed"

"I crystalize real good"

"I shepherd lost sheep"

"I make learning fun"

These probably don't mean a thing to you, right? But Ralph Lauren, the fashion icon, started his whole empire turning scraps of fabric into artistic ties. Called them Polo and sold them to little shops in New York. His purpose? To find beauty and bring it to the world through clothes. Fast forward. Ralph Lauren's worth? Over eight billion dollars. Purpose. Powerful stuff.

"I challenge the status quo and design products that are beautiful and user friendly" did mean the world to Steve Jobs. And he was inspired to produce computers and phones and subsequently much more.

"We change the world through stories" does mean the world to the founders of TED talks.

Your Purpose Statement

Embarking on your Purpose Quest starts with reflection. To get the most out of this journey, follow these steps:

Answer the questions below, taking care to complete each one in two parts: first, brainstorm a list, and then refine it. This dual process is key to uncovering meaningful insights. Resist the urge to take shortcuts. The value lies in the process itself – listing and refining helps you tap into your thoughts and desires. Some exercises may seem repetitive, but that's intentional. Repetition helps solidify your understanding and reveals patterns that can guide you toward your purpose. Now, let's get started.

List 7 words to describe yourself.

Use a thesaurus for each to make sure there isn't a more accurate word. See what we did for Susan earlier in this Chapter.

What makes me tick deep down?

1. What comes really easy to me and not to most others
2. What makes me angry deep down?

3. What makes me happy deep down?
4. What makes me feel alive deep down?
5. What am I afraid of deep down?
6. What makes me tick deep down?
7. What have I been great at since I was a child?

Catching the first thing that comes to mind may well prove valuable. No matter how crazy the words seem, write them down.

These are Susan's answers to serve as an example.

1. What comes really easy to me and not to most others?
2. What makes me angry deep down?
3. What makes me happy deep down?
4. What makes me feel alive deep down?
5. What am I afraid of deep down?
6. What makes me tick deep down?
7. What have I been great at since I was a child?

Susan's answers were:

1. making things simple
2. stupid excuses
3. solving puzzles

4. hearing a beautiful voice

5. getting my time wasted

6. pushing it and taking risks

7. fantasizing and seeing it done

Locate your Enthusiasms

Write down 6 activities you enjoy doing, do well and always have since you were young. Refine and prioritize your list to 3.

Look for the verbs behind your Enthusiasms

Determine what actions are required to do these activities. Look for action verbs like challenge, analyze, connect, create, simplify, promote, present, organize, rather than abstract verbs like caring, helping and showing. Refine and prioritize your list to three.

List Your Natural Talents

(things you were born with and come effortlessly - a talent for art, cooking, teaching, managing, seeing options, peacemaking).

List the things that come naturally, effortlessly and easily to you. Look especially for those natural talents you perhaps take for granted. Maybe people have told you "You have a fantastic memory." "You never give up when you want something." "You can make people comfortable." "You seem to see beyond what people are saying." "You bring out the best in others." "You can sum things up in a flash." Refine and prioritize your list to three.

Look for the Attributes behind Your Talents

(patience, caring, creativity, courage, humor, organizational skills, eloquence, etc.) behind your talents. List 10 adjectives to describe the type of person who embodies these gifts. Describe them only in the positive. Refine and prioritize to 3.

Prioritize your Beliefs

List 5 beliefs, then refine your list to 3.

Prioritize your Faiths

List 5 things you have faith in. Then, refine your list to 3.

What makes you Happy or Excited

List 5 things that make you happy or excited. Then, refine your list to 3.

What Makes you Angry or Sad

List 5 things that make you angry or sad and refine your list to 3

Beneficiaries

Who do you care about?

Outside of your family and friends, who in the world do you care about most? Which segments of society deserve to benefit from your purpose? List as many as you can, then prioritize to three.

Find your Perfect Verb

Susan's perfect verb is "challenge." Others might be: simplify, complicate, empathize, protect, organize, interpret, shepherd, integrate, find, explore, present, bring together, encourage, generate, break, reveal, invent, blend, search out, discover, give, make, create, champion, and change. To name just a few.

Put it all together

Review your notes and refer to the preceding examples. Think of finding your Purpose Statement like solving a puzzle. Moving words around until they complete the following model.

"I" (insert your perfect verb) (insert what you do) for (insert the intended beneficiary) in order that they can (insert benefit). Sometimes the benefit is obvious so you don't need to mention it—like in "I make learning fun."

Aim for as few words as possible: four to eight is enough. Use the preceding examples and "I make learning fun." "I connect people and ideas." "I give women the strength to succeed." "I challenge seniors to imagine wild, new ideas." "I illuminate choices." "I shepherd lost souls." "I make complicated concepts sound simple and interesting." These simple phrases all changed lives dramatically. Including my own.

You will absolutely know when you are getting close. You will feel it. It will be obvious. Some people offer resistance at this point because they think it's too obvious - but it wasn't obvious before.

The simpler the Statement the better. When you watch someone go through this process you can tell by their face as they get close. It relaxes and they light up inside. Many report it's like floating. It's best summed up in this email after one of my seminars. "I woke up this morning and felt like I'd lost forty pounds."

Chapter 27:
A Very Magic Moment

November 2019.

2:15 AM. Johannesburg. Lost baggage line. Twelve-hour delay in London. British Airways disappeared my bags. Gone. Vanished. Forever. I knew it.

I filled in the lost-luggage forms while Robert, the event planner and two assistants waited for me.

"No sweat," Robert said, all smiles. "Just glad you made it. This is Kayla."

A silver-haired woman in a blue gingham shirt and tight white pants with a wide brown belt stroked her magnificent ponytail and leaned forward.

"Watched all your presentations online. Thrilled to finally meet you."

I felt as if my feet had just touched solid ground for the first time since I left my farm in Canada two and a half days earlier.

"Thanks," I managed. "Looks like a shopping trip for a suit, shirt, shoes is on the agenda in the morning."

"It'll be okay. We'll help you." Robert said. "I know the exact spot—not three minutes from the convention center."

Then, this lanky kid in long grey shorts and a Toronto Blue Jays jersey ambles over. A plastic tray in one hand, he offered me the other. "Hi. I'm Denis." His handshake was as warm as his smile.

"Nice shirt." I said.

"Been quite the night," Robert said as he reached onto the tray and handed me a coffee and a bundle of warm foil. "We're still waiting for one more speaker to clear customs. Big name. Flying in from Vegas."

Robert held the coffee while I peeled back the foil. A roast beef sandwich. Steam rising.

"One of the busiest speakers on the circuit."

"I know." I'd read the program.

I bit into the sandwich and sipped the hot coffee.

"Why not go with Kayla and get settled in the car. Shouldn't be much longer."

"Just what the doctor ordered." I held up the cup and the half-eaten sandwich. "Thanks."

By the time we reached the car the sandwich and the coffee were history. Kayla took the packaging and held the back door open for me.

Alone in the back I thought, 'Robert knows where I'm going. This is where I go to sleep.' I shut my eyes and winced at the thought of replacing my clothes in a few hours. The next flight carrying my bags wouldn't arrive until after my speech and there was no way I could go on stage in front of fifteen hundred financial planners at the Nelson Mandela Convention Center in the jeans, Blundstones, a denim shirt and a tweed jacket. My go-to travel uniform. Not exactly keynote speaker chic.

I don't know how long I napped but when I came around I was sprawled across the back seat. I opened my eyes. Denis was at the wheel. I sat up. We were cruising along an empty expressway between brightly lit office towers in downtown Johannesburg.

The person in front of me had a giant white pillow jammed between her head and the window, a makeshift barrier against the fatigue of the long flight. Her arm was wrapped around her shoulder, her wrist exposed. Something gold flashed and caught my eye. She must have heard me shift. She spoke without turning, her voice thick with sleep.

"Thought you don't do red-eyes, Nick," she mumbled, a little smile in her voice.

I smiled to myself, feeling a familiar sense of comfort in our banter. I leaned forward.

"Still sporting the Patek Philippe, Julia," I said, my voice quiet.

"Yep," she replied, still sounding half-asleep. "And I'm still sitting up here, and you're still back there."

A hint of playful challenge in her tone. I couldn't help but chuckle.

Julia's Purpose Statement. "I give women the courage to achieve."

Her speech. "Find your voice. Free your Spirit. Rule your world."

NICHOLAS BOOTHMAN

EARTH ANGELS & MAGIC MOMENTS

Epilogue

We've walked through these pages together, exploring quiet acts of extraordinary kindness that ripple through ordinary days, the seemingly chance encounters that feel like something more, something... purposeful. We've seen how individuals, without capes or fanfare, can embody a selfless spirit, and how life, in its unpredictable dance, sometimes gifts us with moments that defy explanation, those fleeting instances of pure, unadulterated magic.

Now, as you turn this final page, perhaps a new awareness will settle within you, a heightened sensitivity to the subtle currents of compassion that flow around us, often unseen, and a deeper appreciation for those uncanny moments of serendipity that punctuate the mundane.

Keep your senses attuned, because the world is full of unexpected allies and whispers of wonder, and you might just find yourself encountering Earth Angels and

Magic Moments when you least expect it, or witnessing a touch of magic in the most unlikely of places. And who knows? Maybe, in your own unique way, you'll become a source of that light for someone else, a quiet force of good in a world that often needs it most.

The story might end here, but the possibilities? They're just beginning.

NICHOLAS BOOTHMAN

Acknowledgements

This book owes its existence to the invaluable support and contributions of numerous remarkable individuals who, like unexpected gifts, spontaneously entered my life, ignited paths I never could have foreseen, and then, with some exceptions, faded away again.

Among these amazing individuals are Tim Motion, Jane Somerville, José Prazeres, Susan Bolotin, Dick Martin, Rui Gonçalves, Dorothea Helms, Kerri King, Tim Whyte, Margaret Zwart, Sandra Topper, Ross Harvey, Lynda Hill, and Bernard Scrivener.

Thanks to Alexandra Leggat, my editor, for turning a complex manuscript into an entertaining book.

Additionally, I am thankful to those who supported me with their steadfast patience and unwavering radiance, including Mike Freedman, Dr. Claire Murphy, Vesa Villander, Brendan Calder, Sheldon Rudner, John and Lizzie Blackburn, Roderick Stewart, Jason King, Joanna, Kate, and Pippa Boothman, and Thomas and Sandy Pinto Basto.

And Wendy, of course, who always lights the way.

Also by Nicholas Boothman
Spontaneous Success is Everywhere
Convince Them in 90 Seconds or Less
How to Make People Like You in 90 Seconds or Less
How to Make Someone Fall in Love with You in 90 Minutes or Less
The Irresistible Power of Story Speak
Writing Madly - How to Write a Saleable Book in 10 Minute Bursts of Madness

About the Author

Nicholas Boothman is a true Renaissance man who defied convention by reinventing himself five times in 47 years, each time in 24 hours or less.

His journey has taken him from a high school dropout to a fashion photographer with studios on three continents, and then to a bestselling author with nearly 4 million books in print. But that's not all – he's also a motivational speaker who has inspired millions on every continent, and a champion for human potential in rural communities. Amidst all these pursuits, Boothman has nurtured a loving family with his wife of 53 years and raised five children, all while running a thriving working farm.

He has taught his revolutionary techniques of "Spontaneous Success" to thousands of corporations and colleges around the world including the Harvard and London Business schools. His first two books, How to Make People Like You in 90 Seconds or Less and Convince Them in 90 Seconds or Less have been translated into more than 30 languages.